HISTORIC AIRCRAFT WRECKS

—— OF ——
LOS ANGELES COUNTY

G. PAT MACHA

FOREWORD BY PETER STEKEL

THE
History
PRESS

Published by The History Press
Charleston, SC 29403
www.historypress.net

Cover images: Front image of Western Air Express Boeing 247D on Pinetos Peak, January 12, 1937, courtesy of D.D. Hatfield Collection. Back image, left, of Army Air Force C-46A on Pallet Mountain, photo by Pat J. Macha; image of G.P. Macha at AT-6C crash site, circa 1989, photo by Pat J. Macha.

First published 2014

ISBN 978.1.5402.1072.2

Library of Congress Control Number: 2014953185

To those who lost their lives while in military service on behalf of our nation, and to honor those who were aerial first responders lost on search and rescue, firefighting and law enforcement missions in Los Angeles County, California.

CONTENTS

FOREWORD

Pat Macha—author of this book and a companion volume, *Historic Aircraft Wrecks of San Bernardino County*—is a widely respected specialist in California aviation accident history. A retired high school history teacher, Pat is not only the author of five books about aircraft accidents but also a highly sought-after public speaker on the subject of military, commercial and private airplane crashes in the mountains, deserts and seashores of California. His knowledge of this subject is extensive, spanning more than a half century of research and crash site investigations.

As Pat points out in story after story, the causes of airplane accidents can be attributed to a combination of factors, including human, mechanical and structural failures, as well as weather. While it is possible to read about tragic aircraft accidents from the comfort of your armchair and forget they involve real people, that's not so when you read accounts by Pat Macha.

As he emphasizes, these accidents had profound effects on families, parents, siblings and friends. Pat's breadth of knowledge on the details of aviation accidents—when, where and why they occurred—is only exceeded by his depth of compassion for families who must live with the loss or injury of loved ones.

In a nation that is largely unaware of its aviation history, Pat Macha's books help his readers begin to comprehend the heartrending loses and sacrifices made by the men and women serving in our nation's armed forces, as well as the heroic contributions of our aerial first responders in law enforcement, forest service and military.

This book and his Project Remembrance missions testify to Pat's dedicated efforts on behalf of aviation history and of bereaved next of kin.

PETER STEKEL
Author, *Final Flight: The Mystery of a WWII Plane Crash and
the Frozen Airmen in the High Sierra*

ACKNOWLEDGEMENTS

This book would not have been possible without the help and encouragement of many individuals and organizations. They are listed in chronological order, starting when I began researching and documenting aircraft crash sites in Los Angeles County.

1965–73: Fred Beam, Civil Aeronautics Board, Accident Investigator, Los Angeles County Sheriff's Department. Aero Squadron captain Sewell Griggers (RIP); his brother, Lyndell Griggers (RIP); and Civil Air Patrol Squadron 35 members Pat Quinn and Scotty MacGregor, who flew me over many crash sites that I would never found otherwise. I am indebted to United States Forest Service ranger Mike Alt and my longtime hiking partners, brother Chris and sister Cindy Macha. Since 1967, brothers-in-law Bill, Donald, Bob and Herb Lank have been stalwart companions. Aviation historian David D. Hatfield for providing many rare photographs, Don Young and Hawthorne High students Kirk McKewon and Raymond Nelson.

1974–84: Robert "Bob" Koch, USAF; Major C.L. Burrell and Wyn Selwin, both of Civil Air Patrol fame; Jon K. Lawson; David Chichester; Harry Krig, USAF (Ret.); Captain Paul Stebelton, USAF and FAA (Ret.); Michael J. McIntyre; Don Mitchell; David W. Bryan; Greg Gilger; and the Catalina Island Conservancy for facilitating crash site visitations.

1985–95: Bob Bhrule, Civil Air Patrol; Rich Allison (RIP); Francis S. Yarnell; the X-Hunters, Peter Merlin and Tony Moore; Jim Rowan; Joel Bishop; Ben Giebeler (RIP); John Zimmerman; Robert Gates; and Elgin F. "Butch" Gates (RIP), former San Bernardino County sheriff's deputy, who was enthralled by the Mojave's history and its beauty. His newspaper research provided much help regarding aircraft accident stories and histories. Jack Farley Jr., Los Angeles County park ranger, was our guide to the C-119G and C-46A sites on Pallet Mountain.

1996–2014: Joel Bishop; Don Jordan; Roy Wolford (RIP); Tom Gossett (RIP); Bill Gossett; Captain Alan Dow, Civil Air Patrol; Greg Chrisman; Nick Veronico; Trey Brandt; Chris Killian; Marc McDonald; Lewis Shorb; and Jeff Corder, an inspiration regarding next-of-kin issues. Also Project Remembrance Team members Chris LeFave; Ryan Gilmore; Thomas Maloney; David Mihalik; Dennis Richardson; David Lane; Bruce Guberman; Rick Baldridge; Jana Churchwell; Tony Accurso and his daughter, Evelyn; Walt Witherspoon; and Dan and Leslie Catalano. Fellow authors Eric Blehm and Milo Peltzer have encouraged me to pursue my goal of writing this book. Craig Fuller, founder of Aviation Archaeological Investigation & Research (AAIR) and provider of countless accident reports and photos. George Petterson, National Transportation Safety Board investigator (Ret.), master pilot and aviation safety educator, without whose insights and help I would never have had the aerial perspective of numerous crash sites in the San Gabriel Mountains from his beloved Super Cub. Special thanks to William T. Larkins, author and founder of the American Aviation Historical Society (AAHS), who supplied many historic photos used in this edition; to AAHS director Paul Butler for his many hours of help; and to Jeri Bergen, current AAHS president. Special thanks to Ron Funk, webmaster for www.aircraftwrecks.com, who was responsible for scanning and resizing all images used in this book. Also Rudy Loftin, UAL captain (Ret.); San Bernardino County Coroner divers David Van Norman and John Croaker; Jim Blunt; Steve Lawson; Jon Jolly (RIP); and Gary Fabian and his UB88.org team members Captain Kyaa Day Heller, Kendal Raine, John Walker and Captain Ray Arntz, all of whom played key roles during the search effort for Gertrude Tompkins-Silver and in the discovery of the T-33A missing since 1955. The Ken and Laura Whittal-Scherfee family, the Tom Theiler family, the Theresa Theiler Morton family, Gene Ralston, Mike Pizzio, Chris Killian, Colleen Keller and other members of the Missing Aircraft Search Team (MAST) who participated in the last major Santa Monica Bay search effort. Tom Maloney and Dave Mihalik for hundreds of hours of newspaper research assistance. Jerry Boal for sharing his expertise on all things photo related. Jerry Roberts, my commissioning editor for The History

ACKNOWLEDGEMENTS

Press, for his help and encouragement in completing this book project. Finally, I acknowledge my editor and wife, Mary Jane Macha, without whose tireless help this book would not have been completed on time.

I thank my family for encouraging and supporting my avocation and for joining me in fifty-one years of hiking and searching, sometimes risking life and limb in the process. I salute my parents, Charles F. and Mary Francis Macha (RIP). My father served in the Thirteenth Airborne Division, Eighty-eighth Glider Infantry Regiment during World War II, and his aerospace career with Douglas, Lockheed and North American Aviation/Rockwell/ Boeing spanned forty years. From him I learned about aircraft structure and prefix numbers, not to mention a love of everything aerospace history related. My younger brother, Chris, and my sister, Cindy, started hiking with me in the 1960s. Mary Jane, my wife of forty-seven years, has been on the trail with me since we starting dating in 1966. Our son, Patric Joseph, and daughter, Heather Maureen, along with their respective families, have all participated in visiting crash sites in Los Angeles County and beyond. Our favorite place to drive-in camp is Guffy Campground. At 8,300 feet, this beautiful campground is located just six miles off Highway 2, near the mountain community of Wrightwood in the San Gabriel Mountains. On a clear day, visitors can take in the entire expanse of Los Angeles County from this unique outpost in the sky.

INTRODUCTION

The year 2014 marks my fifty-first year of searching for and documenting aircraft crash sites in open-space areas throughout the state of California. I came to this unique avocation while working at a youth camp in the San Bernardino Mountains of Southern California in the summer of 1963. My camp job was hike master, and that included nature walks, day hikes and overnight camping trips into the San Gorgonio wilderness. A highlight of the overnight trips included the ascent of Mount San Gorgonio, the highest peak in Southern California at 11,503 feet. At that time, the prescribed route to the summit was via the Poop Out Hill Trail Head to a bivouac site at Dollar Lake. After a night's rest, we hiked to the summit of "Old Greyback," where the view on a good day could be one hundred miles or more. Following lunch at the top, we reversed our course, picking up our packs and gear at Dollar Lake to begin the trek back to the parking lot at Poop Out Hill, where a stake bed truck would return us to YMCA Camp Conrad in Barton Flats. We averaged eighteen and a half miles in two days on these wilderness treks. Continuous route repetition led me to try another way down from the summit where no trail existed in those years.

On our first descent on the east flank of Greyback, we stumbled upon the crash site of an air force transport plane that I recognized to be a Douglas C-47. Our group was dumbstruck as we surveyed a scene of devastation, where wings, landing gears and engines were interspersed with personal effects, uniforms, shoes, luggage bags and headphone sets. Campers and counselors asked me what happened and when and who was on board? I wanted to know the answers to these questions too. The aluminum structure looked new, bright and shiny. Our star-and-bar national insignia was visible on one of the wings, with "USAF" on the other. I photographed the crash site that day with an Argus C3, a 35mm camera borrowed from my father, from whom my love of everything airplane comes.

I finally did learn the story of the C-47 tragedy from a U.S. Forest Service (USFS) ranger at Barton Flats Station; he also shared with me the locations and stories of eight other aircraft crash sites that he had seen during his long tenure in the San Bernardino Mountains. This ranger had opened a door to the past, and I began the long search that has continued to this day looking for crash sites that are scattered across the mountains, hills and deserts of California. Unlike roadside vehicle accidents, which are quickly cleaned up and forgotten, aircraft wreck sites in remote locations remain largely undisturbed in deep canyons, hidden in forests, overgrown in the chaparral or widely scattered in small parts across vacant desert landscapes where few people venture.

Los Angeles County covers 4,752 square miles, characterized by coastal plains, numerous valleys, a dozen named hills and mountain ranges that include the Santa Monica, Santa Susana, San Gabriel, Sierra Pelona and Verdugo. The highest point in the county is 10,068-foot Mount San Antonio, also known as Mount Baldy, and it is located in the San Gabriel Mountains. Portions of other Transverse Ranges, the extreme southwestern end of the Tehachapi Mountains, the western edge of the Mojave Desert—including the Antelope Valley, with eight named buttes—and a portion of Rosamond Dry Lake all lie within the county. Four major rivers—the Los Angeles, San Gabriel, Rio Hondo and Santa Clara—along with the Newhall Pass and the San Andreas Fault Zone, are important geographic features. Also, within the county of Los Angeles, in an hour's flight off shore, are two of the California Channel Islands, Santa Catalina and San Clemente. A burgeoning population of more than 10 million people is served by interstate highways such as the Christopher Columbus (known as Interstate 10), Interstate 5 and twelve other major freeways—together they make LA a twenty-first-century "autopia." Two harbors (Long Beach and Los Angeles) and three major rail lines, along with LAX, one of the world's busiest airports, make Los Angeles one of the most financially dynamic and diverse counties in all of the United States.

Within this mix of desert, hills, mountains, islands and the Pacific Ocean lie more than 450 aircraft crash sites, including more than a dozen missing planes presumed lost at sea. This book will give the reader a glimpse into aviation accident stories, histories and mysteries that remain today on private and public open space lands, two islands and beneath the Pacific Ocean.

By the mid-1920s and '30s, the combination of climate and undeveloped open space made Los Angeles County the ideal place for airfields, airports and aircraft manufacturing. Many aviation pioneers launched successful businesses here, including Allan Loughead, the founder of Lockheed Aircraft Company, which made Burbank Airport its home. Donald Wills Douglas established Douglas Aircraft Company at Clover Field in Santa Monica. James "Dutch" Kindelberger founded North American Aviation with a factory at what is now LAX. Jerry Vultee built his manufacturing facility at Vultee Field in Downey. John "Jack" Northrop founded Northrop Aircraft Company in Hawthorne at Northrop Field, later known as Hawthorne Municipal Airport. Howard Hughes built his factory and airfield in Culver City.

During the halcyon days of flight in Los Angeles County, small airfields and airstrips abounded, such as Kelly's Airfield, now the site of Hawthorne High School, and thirty-nine other airfields that no longer exist—paved over, built on and now largely forgotten. In the heyday of mass aircraft production from 1940 to 1980, Los Angeles County was the "aerospace capital of America," employing tens of thousands of men and women. Other companies flourished during this time, too, including Garrett Air Research, Fletcher, Parker Hannifin, TRW, Doak and Aerospace Corporation, all of which added to the earning power and prestige of Los Angeles County. In the modern era, Boeing, Raytheon and Northrop Grumman have made their marks here, too, but some manufacturers have relocated to Arizona, Texas, Georgia and elsewhere in the southeastern United States. Nonetheless, the aerospace legacy of innovation and resilience in the twentieth century lives on in new companies like Robinson Helicopters and SpaceX, leading the way into the twenty-first century.

Chapter 1

FLYING INTO THE STORM

The twentieth century got off to a flying start in Los Angeles County, first with balloons carrying passengers on sightseeing flights and later with powered aircraft. Early aviation accidents often involved pilot error, and sometimes power plant or structural failures also were an issue. Stunt flying, wing walking and other daredevil antics did occasionally end in tragedy. Most of these accidents occurred at or near the early airstrips during training flights or air shows.

One of the earliest aviation accidents in Los Angeles County involved a hydrogen-filled balloon called the *American* that launched from Pasadena on Saturday, August 10, 1909, with a pilot and five passengers riding in a wicker basket. The flight departed Tournament Park in Pasadena at 3:00 p.m., rising quickly to an estimated 6,000 feet, and in light winds, the balloon drifted over the snow-covered San Gabriel Mountains and into an arriving storm. The balloon passed by Mount Lowe and then swiftly passed west of Mount Wilson, heading straight toward 6,256-foot Strawberry Peak. With a possible collision eminent, luck carried the *American* around the looming peak, and that's when the pilot pulled the rip cord, releasing gas from the balloon. The result was a hard landing cushioned somewhat by the chaparral on the rugged north slope of the mountain. Amid a snowstorm, shaken and bruised, Captain A.E. Mueller and his passengers hunkered down for the night.

Prior to the flight, Captain Mueller asked everyone to remove any matches they were carrying as a safety precaution, as the hydrogen gas used in the balloon was highly flammable. Fortunately, one of the passengers, Mr. Sidney Cray, found one match in his coat pocket lining, and with that match, they made a campfire that gave the survivors light but little warmth. Snow showers and the sound of thunder added to the trepidation of those who had narrowly escaped serious injury and death. The following morning, the men began their trek down Fern Grotto Canyon. The snow had turned to rain, and after a day of hiking, they were cold, wet and very hungry when they stumbled into Colby's Ranch just before sunset. Luckily for these aeronauts, Mr. Colby was at home.

The weather kept the men with Mr. Colby until Tuesday morning, when they began the long hike to Switzer's Camp, where there was a telephone. Meanwhile, since no trace of the balloon could be found by searchers, many people thought that Captain Mueller and his passengers had perished in the wilds of the San Gabriel Mountains. The aeronauts were saved by a combination of luck, piloting skill and perhaps divine intervention. The wicker basket and the gas bag were eventually recovered and repaired to be used again. The coming age of air transportation had begun, with an inauspicious start.

World War I saw the establishment of flying training schools in the Greater Los Angeles area. Year-round flying was possible here, except for the occasional strong down-slope winds and winter storm fronts that briefly swept the basin. Most people did not consider low coastal clouds and fog to be weather. The stratus clouds would come in at night and burn off by early afternoon near the coastline. The stratus clouds were most common in the months of May, June and from late September through mid-October. Stratus clouds could, however, appear at any time of year when atmospheric conditions were right. These non-storm clouds would be a factor in many aviation accidents in Los Angeles County, except in the sun-drenched, and sometimes windy, Antelope Valley.

When the United States entered World War I in 1917, both Goodrich and Goodyear were building blimps for coastal and convoy protection. The highly successful C-6 was manned by a crew of five and powered by a two-hundred-horsepower Hall-Scott L-6 engine. The 192-foot-long, 42-foot-diameter blimp was filled with 181,000 cubic feet of noncombustible helium. Hanging beneath the gas bag was the car, where the flight crew and engine were housed. The top speed of this early sky ship was sixty miles per hour, and enough fuel was carried for a ten-hour patrol mission.

On September 29, 1920, U.S. Navy (USN) blimp C-6, piloted by Lieutenant Gordon G. McDonald, was engaged in a military exercise know as a "Fleet Problem," which intended to simulate an attack by enemy vessels approaching the West Coast. The C-6 was operating in darkness and fog when the crew became lost, flying well inland from the shoreline it intended to patrol and into the Santa Monica Mountains. The crash occurred west of Laurel Canyon at about 1,250 feet above sea level in an area undeveloped at the time. The thick blanket of chaparral that covered the mountains and low airspeed helped mitigate the impact. Three crewmen were seriously injured, including the pilot, who sustained two broken ankles, while three others escaped with cuts and bruises.

The wreck was mostly removed and scrapped shortly after the accident by a crew of fifty naval personnel. In the spring of 2007, the author attempted to locate this historic accident site, but the exact location could not be determined. Wildfires and encroaching development have erased what little might have remained of the C-6.

On January 18, 1923, the navy experienced another aircraft loss in Los Angeles County that was weather related. This crash occurred on Santa Catalina Island and involved a large Curtiss F-5L flying boat A-3359 that was assigned to VT-2 at North Island Naval Air Station (NAS) in San Diego County. Eyewitnesses saw the flying boat come out of a fog bank, swerve to avoid a sightseeing boat and crash into large rocks on the shoreline at Abalone Point, southeast of the town of Avalon. The crash killed the pilot, Lieutenant Earl B. Brix, and copilot, Lieutenant W.H. Rohrback. One crewman was critically injured, and five others suffered broken bones and severe contusions. It was considered a miracle that anyone survived the impact velocity, estimated to have been about forty miles per hour.

Aircraft could be used for military purposes, for pleasure, as a platform to carry cameras for the growing Hollywood movie industry, to carry passengers, to explore and map remote areas of the world or to transport the U.S. Mail. Mail contracts provided early airlines with much-needed sources of revenue. Banks and businesses relied on mail planes to deliver registered mail containing thousands of dollars in checks and cash. Getting the mail through on time often meant taking risks, such as flying in marginal weather conditions. Instrument or blind flying training and techniques were in their infancy in the 1920s and '30s, but the mail had to get through, sometimes at great risk to pilots and their machines.

Such was the case on October 26, 1927, when a Pacific Air Transport Ryan M-1 mail plane crashed near Castaic just north of the Newhall Pass. The M-1 was en route from the Saugus airstrip, twenty miles north of Burbank Airport in the Santa Clarita Valley, to San Francisco, Portland

The U.S. Navy Curtiss F-5L flying boat that crashed on Catalina Island on January 18, 1923. *G.P. Macha Collection.*

and, finally, on to Seattle. The mail had been trucked to Saugus because of dense fog in Burbank. At the 2:00 a.m. time of takeoff, the weather was deteriorating, and the pilot, Dick Bowman, struggled to climb above the clouds but became disoriented and bailed out at nine thousand feet as his Ryan M-1 spiraled down out of control. The pilot survived with minor injuries, and the next morning, he walked several miles to reach help in Castaic. The wreck of the mail plane was not located until November 6, thanks to a veritable army of volunteer searchers that included many troops of Boy Scouts and resident ranchers and farmers. Why so many volunteers? One motivator might have been the reward offered by Pacific Air Transport. When the wreck of the M-1 was finally located on November 6 in rugged Rattlesnake Canyon northeast of Castaic by L.G. Klein, a construction engineer, he received nothing! Unbeknownst to Mr. Klein, the reward offer had been canceled the previous day. All of the mail was finally recovered and sent on its way, including $750,000 in negotiable bonds.

The fabric-covered M-1 monoplane was powered by the Wright J-4B engine and had a top speed of 125 miles per hour and a range of 400 miles.

FLYING INTO THE STORM

The M-1 was the predecessor of the historic Ryan *Spirit of St. Louis*, flown by Charles Lindbergh across the Atlantic in 1927. Lindbergh was himself an airmail pilot and had to bail out twice during his mail flying career.

On January 2, 1930, three Stinson SM-1 Detroiter aircraft departed Clover Field, now Santa Monica Airport, to film a segment for a movie that required a stunt man to bail out over the Pacific Ocean near Point Fermin on the Palos Verdes Peninsula. Each Stinson had five people on board, including the famous film director Kenneth Hawks and noted cameraman George Eastman. Just as the camera planes were getting into position for the shot about one mile from shore, they suddenly collided, locked together and burst into flames. The death plunge into the ocean was witnessed by renowned pilot Captain Roscoe Turner, who was flying the third Stinson. Two studio-hired speedboats were in position to film from the ocean perspective and to pick up the parachutist, who had not yet jumped. They, too, saw the collision and a cameraman fall clear of the descending wrecks. The passengers and crew of the steamer *Ruth Alexander* also saw the tragedy firsthand, but the ship did not stop because the speedboats had the situation under control. Of the ten fatalities, only six of the bodies were recovered the day of the accident.

All the men aboard the two Stinson SM-1 Detroiters involved in the collision were employed by the Fox Studio Corporation, except for the two pilots. The motion picture they were filming at the time of the accident was never completed. Ironically, the movie was based on the mysterious death of a Belgian multimillionaire aviator who disappeared from an airliner on a flight over the English Channel in 1928. Kenneth Hawks's two brothers, William and Howard, went on to lead successful Hollywood careers as a producer and director, respectively.

The Boeing Model 40 was a successful single-engine biplane that accommodated four passengers within the fuselage, as well as a pilot in the open cockpit aft. Tragedy struck a Pacific Air Transport Boeing Model 40C, NC-5390 mail plane flown by Arthur D. Starbuck, with Charles R. Parmalee riding in the cabin with six bags of mail. They were on the night mail flight from San Diego to Burbank Airport on May 5, 1931, when they encountered stratus clouds and fog that obscured their destination. The roar of the Boeing's Pratt & Whitney 420-horsepower Wasp engine was last heard at 11:25 p.m. near the airport. The wreck of the ill-fated mail plane was found the next morning in the Verdugo Mountains unburned, but both crewmen were dead. The clock in the NC-5390 had stopped at 11:29 p.m. The mailbags were recovered, and the contents were delivered, albeit a day late. The crash site of the Model 40C is located south of La Tuna Canyon

Boeing Model 40C passenger mail plane belonging to Pacific Air Transport, circa 1931. *Courtesy American Aviation Historical Society.*

Boeing Model 40C NC-5390 wrecked in La Tuna Canyon on May 5, 1931. *Courtesy D.D. Hatfield Collection.*

22

on a steep hillside, where a few parts and fittings are all that remain. Not surprisingly, fog was cited as factor in this accident.

The Catalina Wilmington Airline enjoyed considerable success in the early 1930s, partly by using the latest in amphibious aircraft capable of carrying passengers from Long Beach to Hamilton Cove near Avalon on Catalina Island. The Douglas Dolphin proved to be a successful addition to the CWA fleet, but new designs often had different handling traits, and it took some time for pilots to acquire the knowledge to fly their new aircraft safely.

On November 11, 1933, a Dolphin piloted by Walter Siler, CWA's chief pilot, crashed while trying to take off from the Hamilton Cove Seaplane Base. The rough seas may have been a factor in the accident, which seriously injured Mr. Siler and killed both copilot George Baker and CWA vice-president Elliott McFarlane Moore. Mr. Moore was an Annapolis graduate and had served in the U.S. Navy with distinction. He was an advocate for purchasing the Dolphins, and they performed well for CWA, carrying more than thirty-six thousand passengers accident free—until November 11, that is. The Dolphins continued to safely fly the Catalina Channel until late December 1941, when U.S. entrance into World War II ended passenger air service to the island.

George K. Rice was a well-known and very capable pilot for Trans Continental and Western Airlines, later known as Trans World Airlines (TWA). In 1934, Mr. Rice was assigned to fly the Northrop Alpha 3A, an all-metal monoplane powered by the Pratt & Whitney Wasp engine. The Alpha could carry two passengers and 465 pounds of mail within the fuselage, with the pilot still seated aft in an open cockpit. The cruising speed achieved by the Alpha was 145 miles per hour—fast for its day. It was hailed as the first modern airliner.

On November 15, 1934, Rice was flying from Albuquerque, New Mexico, to Burbank Airport in Alpha 3A NC-999Y when he crash-landed on a ridgeline in the Santa Susana Mountains during a blinding rainstorm. Surviving the crash without sustaining serious injuries was miracle in itself. Rescuers were not able to locate the downed Alpha for twelve hours, during which time Mr. Rice stood guard over his cargo of registered mail, valued at $350,000. It was a Los Angeles County sheriff's search aircraft that spotted the Alpha 3A wreck just after sunrise on November 15. The rescuers' hike to the crash site was arduous, but they made it. To recover the mailbags, mules were used, as was a donkey cart to take Mr. Rice off the mountain. Because the Alpha was virtually intact, plans were made to disassemble the wreck and remove it piece by piece. This was accomplished within a few weeks of the accident.

TWA Northrop Alpha 3A lies wrecked in the Santa Susana Mountains. Pilot George K. Rice survived the crash unscathed. *Courtesy Chris Baird via Craig Fuller.*

George K. Rice had a distinguished career with TWA, flying more than 1 million miles until his retirement in 1957. In April 2014, the author's son, Pat J. Macha, and a friend located the now historic Alpha 3A crash site. During their brief visit, respects were paid to the memory of the pioneer mail and passenger pilot.

News of the Alpha crash and the rescue of the pilot caused a sensation in the local news media. The owner of Pacific Aeromotive Corporation, W.E. "Tommy" Thomas, decided to take an aerial look at the Alpha wreck. He invited three of his employees to join him aboard his Waco Model C cabin biplane NC-13065. The Waco departed Burbank on November 17, 1934, in clear weather, but clouds enshrouded the Newhall Pass and the mountains around it. Tommy Thomas was a highly experienced pilot, but in blind flying conditions, it was another story. A witness near the Alpha crash scene reported seeing the Waco descend out of the clouds and crash, disintegrating when it struck Head Gate Mountain near the Los Angeles Aqueduct spillway. Tommy Thomas, Roy W. Kidd, F.M. Matthews and twenty-two-year-old Dorothea Benham died instantly in this accident in which clouds, and not a storm, were a factor.

As the demand for U.S airmail and passenger service increased, aircraft manufacturers began offering new designs that would revolutionize air travel

FLYING INTO THE STORM

The Waco Model C cabin biplane that crashed on Head Gate Mountain, killing all three men and one woman on November 17, 1934. *Courtesy D.D. Hatfield Collection.*

around the world. Boeing was in the leadoff position with a twin-engine all-metal airliner that could carry ten passengers, baggage and four hundred pounds of mail. The Boeing 247D had a cruising speed of 189 miles per hour and a range of 745 miles while flying at an altitude of 12,000 feet. The service ceiling of the 247D was an incredible 25,400 feet. Seventy-five of these airliners were built before Lockheed and Douglas entered the competition with new designs of their own.

United Air Lines (formerly Pacific Air Transport) purchased several of these new transports for use in its growing network of routes. On December 27, 1936, Boeing 247D NC-13355 departed San Francisco Municipal Airport at 5:33 p.m. with a flight crew of three and nine passengers bound for Union Air Terminal in Burbank. The flight time en route was about two hours, but a storm front producing heavy rains and strong winds impeded the progress of the 247D, and at 7:09 p.m., the pilot radioed Burbank to say they would arrive about seven minutes late; seconds later, another call came in, with just "wait a minute" and then silence. The pilots must have seen the mountains in their flight path and pulled up in a desperate effort to avoid

25

The Boeing 247D flown by Western Air Lines, similar to the one that crashed on Los Pinetos Peak on January 12, 1937. *Courtesy American Aviation Historical Society.*

the crash. The Boeing 247 was already flying into Rice Canyon on the north slope of the rugged Santa Susana Mountains when it struck oak trees and plunged into the canyon bottom, killing all on board.

Within minutes of the last radio call from the 247D, an alert was sent to airports in Santa Barbara and Ventura Counties, hoping that the UAL airliner might have become lost and was heading their way. Reports flooded in from people claiming to have heard engine sounds in the clouds and darkness as far away as Palo Alto, Coalinga, Sandberg, Quail Lake and Ventura. By 10:30 p.m., NC-13355 was declared missing, and an extensive search effort was launched the next morning. On Tuesday, December 29, a rancher rounding up stray cattle stumbled upon parts of the 247D. He called down the hill to his wife and asked her to join him. Together they found the main impact of the smashed but unburned airliner that they had read about in their morning newspaper. Seeing that no one remained alive, the couple climbed higher on the mountain and lit a fire to attract searchers.

A recovery team arrived that afternoon, battling continuing rain, steep terrain and mud. They used high lines to move the bodies to a ridge top. Packhorses removed the remains of all twelve passengers and crew to a nearby roadway. The body of one of the passengers received special attention because he was a diamond broker and often carried thousands

The fuselage of United Air Lines Boeing 247D NC-13355 in Rice Canyon. All twelve passengers and crew died in this December 27, 1936 weather-related accident. *Courtesy D.D. Hatfield Collection.*

of dollars in diamonds on his person in a specially designed belt. In spite of the best efforts by the coroner, deputy sheriffs and other volunteers, no diamonds were ever found or reported. Among those killed aboard the Boeing 247 were wealthy socialites Mr. and Mrs. Edward T. Ford of San Marino; Miss Yvonne Trego, the UAL stewardess who was remembered for both her charm and cheerfulness; and experienced pilots Edwin W. Blom and Robert McLean, the copilot, whose wife was expecting their first child. The crash of NC-13355 would be the first of three airliner losses that were soon to follow in 1937 and 1938.

The cause of this accident was attributed to pilot error, descending too soon when he had not yet entered the San Fernando Valley. Also complicit was a winter storm, as well as darkness that impaired the pilots' ability to see roadway lights or the flashing aviation beacon light in the Newhall Pass. The Newhall Pass would claim dozens more aircraft in the years to come.

Western Air Express was also an operator of five Boeing 247D aircraft. One of these was NC-13315, which departed Salt Lake City, Utah, early on the morning of January 12, 1937, with ten passengers and a crew of three en route to the Union Air Terminal in Burbank, with a stop in Las Vegas, Nevada. The pilot, Captain William W. Lewis, was cleared to proceed to his destination at 9:00 a.m. local time, with the proviso that Palmdale or Long Beach be used as alternates if the weather were bad in the Newhall Pass area. When the 247D reached Saugus at 10:50 a.m., clouds obscured the Newhall Pass, causing Captain Lewis to continue toward Burbank using instruments and radio range transmissions. He began his descent from 7,000 feet to 5,500 feet, lowering his landing gear and wing flaps in preparation for landing. Captain Lewis then radioed Burbank that he expected to land at 11:06 a.m., but moments later, he radioed again, indicating that ice was building up on the wings of NC-13315 and that he was encountering severe turbulence as well. Flying on instruments and trying to follow intermittent radio range signals, Captain Lewis realized that he was east of his intended course and over mountainous terrain. Seconds later, he saw a mountain ridge covered by chaparral just as his left wing tip struck the terrain, causing the 247D to crash, sliding 125 feet before spinning around and coming to a sudden stop.

The Western Air Express 247D had crashed on the side of Pinetos Peak at 3,550 feet above sea level, remaining remarkably intact. There was no post-impact fire, but the force of the crash killed passenger James A. Braden instantly. Four others who were critically injured would die in the following days, including the famous African explorer Martin Johnson. His wife, Osa, survived with a broken leg and other serious injuries. Copilot Clifford P. Spence, the solitary crew fatality, died of internal injuries and a skull fracture. All other passengers and crew were injured, including flight attendant Esther Jo Conner, who sustained a fractured ankle. Heroically, passenger Arthur S. Robinson hiked and crawled more than four miles to reach the Olive View

Sanatorium near the town of San Fernando, where he told the medical staff that help was urgently needed at the ridge-top crash site. Mr. Robinson was himself suffering from exposure, shock, lacerations and bruises.

Accident investigators from the Department of Commerce determined that a combination of factors were in play, including rain, icing conditions, turbulence and failure by the pilot to maintain an altitude that would have enabled his aircraft to clear the high terrain prior to descending into the San Fernando Valley for landing.

Salvage operations were undertaken during the first quarter of 1937 during which 98 percent of NC-13315 was removed, but in 2010, Ron Kraus and a group of friends scoured the crash site, finding that 1–2 percent of the Boeing 247 still remains on Pinetos Peak, concealed in the tall grasses and partly buried on the westernmost ridgeline of the San Gabriel Mountains.

On January 29, 1937, a flight of three Grumman F2F-1 U.S. Navy biplane fighters assigned to VF-3B on the USS *Ranger* departed North Island Naval Air Station in San Diego County for a flight to Alameda Naval Air Station in the San Francisco Bay area. The flight was uneventful until it encountered stormy weather north of Los Angeles in the vicinity of the Tejon Pass. Flying in the clouds and fearful of colliding with the mountains that line old Highway 99 (Interstate 5), the pilot of F2F-1 Bu No 90654, William H.

A dusting of snow covers Western Air Express Boeing 247D NC-13315 on Los Pinetos Peak as a bystander looks into the cockpit. *Courtesy D.D. Hatfield Collection.*

McClure, elected to bail out. He landed in rough country near a roadway and was rescued. His squadron mates continued on to their destination, landing safely, but were exhausted following their tumultuous flight. When the weather cleared, the crashed Grumman F2F-1 fighter was nowhere to be found. Weeks passed until on February 20, 1937, a rancher found the mangled remains of the stubby little Grumman fighter. Due to the remote crash site location and the condition of the wreckage, the navy made no attempt to salvage the F2F-1. Although wildfires have recently burned in the crash area, it is believed that remnants of the little Grumman survive in situ.

Navy seaplane or flying boat operations based at North Island Naval Station in San Diego County often used San Clemente Island for practice bombing and patrol training flights. This was the case on February 2, 1938, when two Consolidated PBY-2 Catalina flying boats assigned to Long Range Patrol Squadron Eleven (VP-11) collided while flying at night and in clouds. The two PBYs were participating in a fleet exercise when the collision occurred, killing eleven crewmen, although only seven bodies of the eleven were found. In addition, three seriously injured survivors were rescued from the debris-littered Pacific Ocean southwest of San Clemente Island.

The Super Electra was an all-metal eleven-passenger airliner that included a crew of three and could cruise at 216 miles per hour with a range of 1,700 miles. This design, advanced for its day, would serve not only as an airliner but also as a light bomber. First ordered by the Royal Air Force in 1938, it would also serve with the United States Army Air Force (USAAF), U.S. Navy, Canada, China, New Zealand and Australia during World War II known, alternatively, as the Hudson, A-29, AT-18 and PBO-1. Northwest Airlines purchased eleven of the airliner version, but following three fatal accidents, the type was retired by Northwest and replaced by the slower and larger Douglas DC-3.

Weather was a factor in the loss of a speedy Lockheed Model 14H, Super Electra NC-17394, operated by Northwest Airlines on May 16, 1938. The circumstances of this tragic accident share similar factors with earlier airliner losses: weather, mountainous terrain along the flight path and human error. NC-17394 departed Union Air Terminal at Burbank Airport on 1:40 p.m. on a delivery flight to Chicago, Illinois, via Las Vegas, Nevada, and St. Paul, Minnesota. The Super Electra was piloted by Sidney Willey of Lockheed Aircraft Corporation, and the copilot was Fred Whittemore, vice-president of Northwest Airlines. Guest passengers included Mrs. Carl Squier, wife of the Lockheed Corporation vice-president; Miss Lolla Totty, a Lockheed secretary; and Northwest Airlines secretary Evelyn Dingle. Also on board

FLYING INTO THE STORM

A Lockheed Super Electra similar to the one lost on May 16, 1938. *Courtesy American Aviation Historical Society.*

were Northwest Airlines engineer Henry W. Salisbury; his wife, Betty Clare Salisbury; and their two children, two-year-old Richard and three-month-old Judith.

The flight path took the Super Electra through the Newhall Pass, where the pilot turned northeast, following the highway to Palmdale in the Antelope Valley. Clouds obscured the route. It was later thought that the pilot was trying to stay below the clouds, scud-running his way to the blue skies reported over Palmdale. As the terrain rose, the clouds and mountains became one, and the Super Electra, just slightly off course, was flying blind into mountainous terrain. It impacted on the southwest slope of Stroh Peak. When radio contact with NC-17394 was lost, a search effort was initiated. As the afternoon progressed, clouds enshrouded the crash site, limiting search efforts.

On Wednesday, May 18, Walter Peterson, a rancher who lived in Mint Canyon, followed a hunch and found the missing Super Electra on the southwest slope of Stroh Mountain. From what Mr. Peterson saw, he knew that no one could have survived such a crash. He then hiked down the mountain and reported what he had found to the forest service ranger at Mint Canyon Station. When rescue crews arrived at the accident scene that afternoon, they began the grim task of recovering the bodies of those on board. Some of the victims had been ejected from the fuselage still strapped in their seats, while others remained entangled within the wreckage. One engine was catapulted over the ridgeline, coming to rest almost half a mile from the point of impact. A wristwatch found at the scene had stopped at 2:07 p.m., pegging the likely

The wreckage of Northwest Airlines Super Electra on Sierra Pelona Ridge; nine passengers and crew members perished in the crash. *Courtesy D.D. Hatfield Collection.*

time of the crash. Nearby, rescuers found the body of two-year-old Richard Salisbury still clutching his partly burned teddy bear.

An investigation revealed that in the last moments of the flight, the pilot was apparently climbing in an effort to avoid a ridge that he then struck with a glancing blow, causing the Super Electra to bounce and crash in flames on a second ridge only one hundred yards from the top of Stroh Peak. Eight other aircraft would crash on Sierra Pelona Ridge with fatal results in the clouds and storms of later years while trying to follow a roadway through the mountains that is now State Highway 14.

As the 1930s drew to a close, Los Angeles County aircraft manufacturers were experiencing a boom in orders for fighters, bombers, transports and training aircraft. New airfields were being built, and a new generation of airliners was starting to appear, carrying passengers farther, faster and in more comfort and safety. The Douglas DC-Series built in Santa Monica at Clover Field and later at Dougherty Field in Long Beach, along with the Lockheed Loadstar and Constellation series manufactured by Lockheed in Burbank, would lead the way into the next decade, bringing tens of thousands of new arrivals to join a rapidly growing workforce that would make Los Angeles County a key part of the arsenal of democracy during World War II and into the Cold War era that would follow.

Chapter 2
THE WINGS OF WAR

Few people today know that in and around the continental United States, from 1941 to 1945, more than twenty-five thousand military airmen and women were killed in flight training, testing, ferrying, transporting or patrolling our skies and shorelines just prior to and during World War II. In California alone, there were 8,348 accidents involving U.S. Army Air Corps and U.S. Army Air Force aircraft. No exact number of U.S. Navy, Marine Corps or Coast Guard accidents are currently available, but they are estimated to be about half that of the U.S. Army. The U.S. Navy loss rates reflect the number of aircraft assigned to or passing through California. The U.S. Army conducted the majority of military aviation operations within California during World War II.

By 1940, Southern California was the fastest-growing center for aircraft manufacture in the United States. The weather was ideal for year-round flying, land suitable for airports and factories was available and railroad and port facilities made transporting raw materials easy. The population was growing rapidly, guaranteeing a viable workforce. Douglas, Hughes, Lockheed, North American, Northrop and Vultee were all to become aviation giants during World War II. The Greater Los Angeles cities of Santa Monica, Long Beach, Inglewood, Hawthorne, Burbank and Downey became synonymous with aircraft construction. Consolidated and Ryan, based in San Diego, added to our aircraft production capability. Orders poured in, initially from European countries facing invasion by the Axis powers of Italy and Germany. Orders also came from China, already at war with Japan. In addition, Thailand, Turkey and Brazil were buying U.S.-built warplanes. The United States Army Air Corps, U.S. Navy and Marine Corps were beginning to modernize their aviation elements with the latest fighters, bombers, transports, trainers and all manner of other aircraft types.

Our military needed new air bases for training, testing and housing first-line operational squadrons. Los Angeles County had the open, undeveloped spaces. On the western Mojave Desert and in Antelope Valley, the army had Muroc Army Air Field (AAF) in operation. Used initially as a bombing and gunnery range, later it became a well-known operational training base supporting B-24 and P-38 flight operations. Palmdale and Grey Butte Army Air Fields served as auxiliary and emergency landing fields. War Eagle Field was home to Polaris Fight Academy, a contract company that specialized in training cadet pilots from Great Britain and Canada. Liberty and Victory practice fields were satellites of War Eagle Field.

In the Metro Los Angeles area, Van Nuys Army Air Field, located in the San Fernando Valley, was a P-38 training base. Grand Central Airport in Glendale was home to Timm Aircraft Company and Cal-Aero Technical Institute, becoming an operational Army P-38 fighter interceptor base and joining Lomita Fighter Strip in Torrance in the air defense roll. The U.S. Navy established Reeves Naval Air Station on Terminal Island in 1941. It was renamed Terminal Island NAS in 1944, and besides paved runways, the base also had ramps to accommodate flying boats, float planes and amphibious aircraft. The navy built an airfield on San Clemente Island in 1936 that remained active until 1945. Mines Field near the El Segundo, Lennox and Inglewood areas became Los Angeles Metropolitan Airport in the 1940s, and with later development, it would become Los Angeles International Airport. LAX was home to the El Segundo Division of Douglas Aircraft Company and North American Aviation (NAA). Jack Northrop Field in nearby Hawthorne was home to the Northrop Corporation. Douglas Aircraft Company had a large manufacturing facility at Long Beach Airport that dwarfed the company's original home at Clover Field in Santa Monica. Clover Field/Santa Monica Airport is the oldest continually operating airport in Los Angeles County. Vultee Aircraft Company began manufacturing at the old EMSCO airfield in Downey in 1936, later changing the name to Vultee Field.

With the increased volume of air traffic over Los Angeles County, a dramatic spike in aviation accidents was not unexpected, as training activities, flight tests, ferry flights and routine patrols ramped up the odds for mishaps and serious incidents. Training losses sometimes included stall and spin, midair collisions and weather-related accidents. The Vultee BT-13 basic trainer recorded twenty-seven open-space accidents in which the aircraft was heavily damaged or completely destroyed, often with loss of life.

From 1940 to 1945, the mainland, mountainous and desert areas of Los Angeles County would claim more than sixty-five military aircraft. One early loss was that of a navy Curtiss SOC-1 Seagull observation aircraft, which could be flown on floats to facilitate catapult launches from cruisers or battleships. Also, the floats could easily be exchanged for wheels and used when operating from shore bases. On January 10, 1941, a wheel-equipped SOC-1 Bu No 9878 was en route from the Oakland Naval Air Reserve Base in the San Francisco Bay area to Reeves Field in Long Beach, California, when the pilot, Ensign Frank P. Blackmore, USNR, encountered rough weather near historic Shea's Castle, about twenty miles west of Lancaster in the Antelope Valley. Seeing mountains and hills appear through breaks in the clouds, Ensign Blackmore ordered his mechanic in the back seat to bail out. Once Aviation Machinist Mate Third Class Gilbert M. Thompson jumped, his pilot followed. Both men landed safely as their Seagull crashed and burned a half mile west of the castle. Another SOC-1 that Ensign Blackmore was following arrived safely at Reeves Field in spite of the prevailing weather conditions.

Another early but fatal loss involved a USAAF North American Aviation AT-6 Texan advanced trainer flying from Muroc Army Air Field on the morning of June 24, 1941. The pilot was First Lieutenant Jesse K. Jackson, and his passenger was Staff Sergeant Fred L. Pankey. The weather was clear, and the winds were light as AT-6 40-2137 flew across the San Gabriel Mountains toward a saddle between 5,603-foot Mount Lowe and 5,742-foot Mount Markham. Several persons reported hearing the roar of the six-hundred-horsepower Pratt & Whitney R-1340 as it echoed across the ridgelines and into deep canyons before it collided with a telephone line that was strung across the flight path. The collision caused the AT-6 to crash, plunging into remote and rugged Rubio Canyon and killing both men on board. The crash site was located by telephone linesmen on the afternoon of the twenty-fourth after finding the severed line and seeing wreckage in the canyon below them. A Los Angeles County sheriff's posse recovered the bodies of the crew on June 25, but the wreckage remained largely intact until it was partly salvaged by a metal scrapper in the 1950s. Forest fires, followed by heavy rains, have caused landslides in Rubio Canyon that have buried most, but not all, of 40-2137.

The crash site of army air force T-6 Texan trainer 40-2137 in upper Rubio Canyon, circa 1941. *USAF official via AAIR.*

North American Aviation AT-6 Texan trainers in formation, circa 1950. The AT-6 was also known as the SNJ in navy and marine service. Seven crashed in Los Angeles County between 1940 and 1960. *Courtesy William T. Larkins.*

The Lockheed P-38 Lightning fighter sustained more than forty-five losses within Los Angeles County during World War II. Most of these were on familiarization and combat tactics training flights, but a few were lost on test and delivery flights, too. The Lightning was an aircraft that almost every person in World War II–era Los Angeles could identify because of its unique twin-boom design.

One notable P-38 open-space loss occurred at Catalina Island on April 30, 1942, when a young U.S. Army Air Force pilot, Second Lieutenant Walter F. Lichtenberger, assigned to the Ninety-fourth Fighter Squadron at March Field in Riverside County, experienced loss of power in his port engine and attempted to make an emergency landing at the island's airport. In doing so, he slowed his Lightning down too much and crashed on a small hill north of the landing field. Because the P-38F remained largely intact, it was hoped that the pilot had survived, but G forces on impact proved to be too much for his body to withstand. The wreckage of P-38F 41-7498 was disassembled and mostly removed, as so much of the airframe could be usefully recycled for spare parts. The author visited this historic micro site in recent years and was surprised to find parts with the Lockheed prefix numbers still intact.

The disappearance of USAAF major William T. Nunn on April 6, 1943, in Vultee BT-13A 41-11497 occurred while en route from San Bernardino Air Depot to Merced Army Air Field. Major Nunn departed at 3:35 p.m. with a choice of flying through the Cajon Pass and proceeding across the Western Mojave desert to the Sandberg Pass near Lebec and over the Tejon

The USAAF Lockheed P-38F 41-7498 wreck near Buffalo Springs on Catalina Island. *G.P. Macha Collection.*

Pass summit or by flying westerly along the San Gabriel Mountains to the Newhall Pass and then turning north to the Sandberg Pass. The route was the pilot's choice, and he was not required to specify which one he had selected. Low clouds covered the Los Angeles Basin to three thousand feet, and scattered clouds were common above three thousand feet feet.

When Major Nunn failed to arrive at Merced AAF as scheduled, a search was launched; it was delayed until April 10 due to poor weather conditions. Four army airfields participated in the search effort, which spanned only four days but included 140 hours of aerial searching. There was a war in progress, and the war effort came first. However, notices were posted at March AAF, San Bernardino AAF, Muroc AAF and Merced AAF that pilots should be on the lookout for Major Nunn's missing BT-13A, with its high-visibility color scheme: the wings and tail were painted a bright orange-yellow, and the fuselage was painted true blue.

As the months passed, the mystery deepened, especially after the winter snows had melted. Deer season in the San Gabriel Mountains opened in mid-October and continued into mid-December. On December 12, 1943, two hunters struggling to track a six-point buck on the rugged north slope of 5,075-foot Mount Lukens spotted the smashed wreckage of the missing BT-13A, with the partially mummified remains of the pilot still inside the cockpit. The hunters hiked down to the Big Tujungta Road and notified the authorities. Lieutenant Sewell Griggers of the Los Angeles County Sheriff's Department (LACSD) lead a posse up the mountain to the 4,600-foot level to recover the remains of Major Nunn. This mission was accomplished on October 13, 1943. It was speculated at the time that Major Nunn had tried to fly a westerly course to the Newhall Pass but had become lost in clouds, and he may have tried to turn back when he flew into the north face of Mount Lukens.

In the fall of 1998, the author hiked to the crash site of this BT-13A 41-11497 along with his son, brother and nephew. Salvagers, forest fires and rock falls have diminished what remains of the famed Vultee basic trainer. Since there was no post-impact fire, orange-yellow and true blue paint, though faded, were still recognizable on many of the remaining parts. Cockpit instruments and the fabric used to cover the moveable control surfaces had also survived in a place few people ever venture.

Fog and clouds were not a factor in another Vultee BT-13A loss that occurred on November 11, 1943. This accident did not take place in the high mountains or in a remote location. This ill-fated flight began at the Lomita Fighter Strip, now Torrance Airport (Zamperini Field), on a sunny

Captain Sewell F. Griggers and his Los Angeles County Sheriff's Department airplane crash site map. *Courtesy Sewell F. Griggers.*

afternoon. Second Lieutenant Charles C. Zwick and Second Lieutenant Frank H. Huelsbush were to practice their instrument flying skills. The USAAF accident report states that as 41-1197 was climbing to a suitable altitude to begin instrument instruction, the aircraft stalled and spun into the ground on the Chadwick Seaside School located on the Palos Verdes Peninsula at 800 feet above sea level. The BT-13A crashed on an open-space part of the school grounds, where it burst into flames, killing both

The Vultee BT-13, a classic World War II–era basic trainer, is similar to many of those lost within Los Angeles County from 1941 to 1945. *Courtesy American Aviation Historical Society.*

pilots instantly. If this was not tragic enough for the families who had lost their sons, the Zwick family had lost another pilot son one month earlier. Lieutenant Leland C. Zwick was killed at the Lomita Fighter Strip in an accident on October 9, 1943. Lieutenant Zwick's P-38G 42-13478 fighter lost an engine on takeoff, causing it to crash and burn at the northwest end of the runway. Today, a memorial marker honors the Zwick brothers in their hometown of La Canada Flintridge in Los Angeles County.

Mechanical failures, human error, storm clouds and fog are not the only factors in aircraft accidents. High winds and the turbulence they create can be significant contributors in the loss of aircraft, especially when one airplane is towing another.

On January 31, 1943, a USAAF Douglas C-53 Sky Trooper 42-15537 departed Van Nuys Army Air Field in the San Fernando Valley en route to Victorville AAF in San Bernardino County. The departure of 42-15537 had been delayed for several days because of weather conditions along the flight path. Once conditions seemed to improve, Flight Officer Wilbur W. Boyd elected to depart Van Nuys towing a Waco CG-4A glider, 42-46327, with Flight Officers Henry L. Greenfield and James K. Rollins. The rest of the

C-53 crew included copilot Flight Officer Neil W. Rise, Technical Sergeant Charles E. Burnett and passengers Private David P. O'Conner, Private First Class Stewart L. Nengel and Staff Sergeant Robert Edelman.

Once Flight Officer Boyd cleared the San Fernando Valley, he encountered more clouds than blue sky, and ice was starting to build up on the wings and tails of both the C-53 and the CG-4A. Soon, both aircraft were flying enshrouded in clouds and covered by a thickening blanket of ice. Severe turbulence made controlling the tandem flight extremely difficult. Then the unimaginable happened: the empennage and tail separated from the C-53 fuselage, throwing Private First Class Nengel, Private O'Conner and Staff Sergeant Edelman into space. Each man was able to pull his D-ring, deploying the parachutes, but they were already too close to the mountainous terrain, so all three men were critically injured upon landing. The C-53 flight crew had no chance to bail out, and they plunged to their deaths in the cockpit section of their aircraft. At the same time, Flight Officer Greenfield saw the tow rope go straight down into the clouds and immediately pulled the release lever that allowed him to fly unfettered, but ice on the CG-4A wings forced both pilots to bail out as the Waco spiraled downward. Landing in rough terrain, they sustained minor injuries, but their glider crashed into a steep canyon wall and was completely destroyed.

Although this tragic accident occurred over a remote section of mountains and valleys northwest of the small community of Castaic, it did not go unobserved. Local rancher and farmer Norman C. Winkler and his nine-year-old daughter, Marylynn, saw three parachutes coming down about five miles northwest of where they lived. Not having telephone service, Mr. Winkler, with his daughter at his side, began hiking overland in an effort to find the three other airmen and render assistance if needed. The weather was cold, with a light rain falling, the ground was muddy and the terrain was uneven. The trek required several hours before they finally found three army men in very serious condition with contusions, broken bones and in traumatic shock.

Norman Winkler talked to the men, covering them with a parachute and then building a fire before he set off to look for other survivors. Mr. Winkler spread two parachutes out on the ground to make an "X" in the hope of attracting the attention of any aerial searchers. He told Marylynn to stay and comfort the injured men and to keep the fire going as best she could. Fortunately, late in the afternoon, a small plane flew over and spotted the parachutes and smoke from the campfire.

Marylynn Winkler (left) with her sister, Barbara, circa 1943. *Courtesy Marylynn Winkler Butters.*

When Norman Winkler returned from his hike to the fatal scene at the C-53 cockpit section, he began to make stretchers that would be needed when the rescuers arrived. The conditions of Staff Sergeant Edelman and Private First Class Nengel worried both Marylynn and her father. At dusk, the first members of the Los Angeles County Sheriff's Department rescue team arrived. At that point, Private O' Conner, though injured, was able to walk on his own. The rescuers used horses to recover the survivors, and Mr. Winkler and his daughter rode out as well. When they reached a road, vehicles were used to get the injured to a hospital, and the Winklers were driven home, arriving at about midnight. Late that same afternoon, both glider pilots were found alive and without serious injuries. They were rescued by Lieutenant Holbrook of the Headquarters Company, 174th Infantry Regiment, and taken directly back to Victorville AAF.

The next day, the grim task of recovering the bodies of the rest of the crew began, and armed troops were stationed at both the Waco CG-4A and Douglas C-53 crash sites until the initial salvage efforts were completed. Some of the wreckage was removed in early February 1943, but because of the widely scattered nature of the accident scene, about 10 percent of the C-53 still remains on the private land where it crashed. Even though the CG-4A was hardly salvaged, it was burned over several times in the ensuing years, and it's a micro site today.

Sadly, Staff Sergeant Robert Edelman succumbed to his injuries within a few weeks of the accident. Private First Class Stewart L. Nengel required many months' stay in a hospital before he returned to active duty, but it

Right: Private First Class Stewart L. Nengel, survivor of the Douglas C-53 Skytrooper crash on January 31, 1943. *Courtesy Denise Robinson Bartow.*

Below: Pat J. Macha holds part of an aileron from the ill-fated Douglas C-53 Skytrooper that crashed on January 31, 1943. *Photo by G.P. Macha.*

Pat J. Macha with a section of Douglas C-53 rudder assembly. *Photo by G.P. Macha.*

would take several years for him to fully recover from his injuries. During that time, he corresponded with Marylynn Winkler. Marylynn became a celebrity in the weeks and months following the accident. She received a letter from Lieutenant General H.H. "Hap" Arnold, commanding general of the U.S. Army Air Forces, including this commendation: "All of us in the Army Air Forces are very proud of your heroic action." Marylynn was featured in *Calling All Girls*, a magazine published during the war years for young girls, and her story was featured on a radio program hosted by Gene Autry.

As the years passed, Marylynn grew up, married and raised a family of her own. She continued to live in the same area as her childhood home. During this time, contact with Stewart Nengel was lost, but her story and that of her father was not forgotten.

In the fall of 2011, the author was contacted by Denise Robinson-Bartow, the granddaughter of Stewart Nengel, who expressed an interest in visiting Los Angeles County to see the C-53 crash site and meet Marylynn Winkler-Butters. In 2012, an effort was made to locate both crash sites of the C-53 and the Waco CG-4A. Thanks to the efforts of Project Remembrance Team member Marc McDonald and a cooperative property owner, Francine Rippy, both sites were located. On March 31, 2012, Denise and her mother, Ann Nengel-Robinson, were escorted by members of the Project Remembrance Team to meet Marylynn Winkler-Butters and her son, Gary. Joining them was guide and gatekeeper Francine Rippy. Following an emotional meeting at the home of Marylynn, our group caravanned to the C-53 crash site, where scattered wreckage was viewed by all in attendance.

It had been sixty-nine years since Marylynn had visited this one-time scene of sadness and devastation. The oak trees under which the injured survivors had lain were still there, surrounded by a peaceful meadow in an area where development has yet to encroach. Photos were taken, a few keepsakes were collected and time was spent reflecting and reminiscing about the events of January 31, 1943. As gathering clouds of a weak winter storm front approached, we returned to Maylynn's home for snacks and farewells. Stewart Nengel's fragile health prevented him from traveling, but his daughter and granddaughter made sure that he would have plenty of photos to see and a few parts of the C-53 to hold in his hands that had pulled his lifesaving parachute D-ring so long ago.

The year 1944 was the peak one for World War II military aircraft losses in Los Angeles County. More than forty army, navy and marine aircraft crashed in open-space areas, killing more than sixty pilots, aircrew and passengers. The February 24, 1944 loss of Lockheed PV-1 Ventura Bu No 49467 on Sierra Pelona Ridge, near the small community of Acton, killed four civilian employees of Lockheed Aircraft Company as they were conducting a pre-delivery test flight. The PV-1 was en route from Burbank Airport to Palmdale Airport on the Mojave Desert when

From left to right: Francine Rippy, Denise Robinson Bartow, Ann Robinson and Marylynn Winkler-Butters at the C-53 crash site on March 31, 2012. *Photo by G.P. Macha.*

A Lockheed PV-1 Ventura medium bomber, similar to that flown by Martha Dory's husband on February 24, 1944. *Courtesy American Aviation Historical Society.*

the pilot, George T. Dory, entered a line of storm clouds that obscured Hauser Mountain and the descending ridges around it. Tragically, Mr. Dory was just sixty-five feet too low when his Ventura struck a cloud-enshrouded ridge at 4,840 feet mean sea level (MSL). All on board died instantly, just moments before reaching mostly clear skies over the Mojave Desert.

Following the passage of the storm front and the melting of a light snowfall, the bodies of the crew were recovered, and the wreckage was partially salvaged; however, parts of the wings and fuselage were buried on site. On May 27, 1944, Martha Dory, wife of the PV-1 pilot, had a memorial marker placed just above the crash site where her beloved husband died. In part, it is inscribed, "The Wings of God Took Up His Flight, So Long, My Guy." It is signed "MARTHA." Mrs. Dory's memorial was unique for the time, being one of the first placed at or near a fatal air crash site in Los Angeles County.

The ridges and peaks of the Sierra Pelona would claim more aircraft in the years to come; some of these errant planes would come to a catastrophic end very near the PV-1 crash site, all while flying in the clouds, with many trying to follow State Highway 14 corridor from the Los Angeles Basin east to the Great Mojave Desert and beyond.

The winter storm season can be most intense in Southern California from January through mid-March. On March 20, 1944, a severe winter storm was lashing Southern California with heavy snowfall in the San Gabriel Mountains and pouring rains over the Los Angeles Basin. Into this inhospitable mix came USAAF Curtiss C-46A 41-12363 en route from Wickenburg, Arizona, to Long Beach, California. On board were a crew of three and a representative of the Curtiss-Wright Aircraft Company. The mission was described, in the accident report, as a routine training flight. At about 10:20 a.m., the pilot of the C-46A, Second Lieutenant Spence E. Gawthrop, called Long Beach tower to say that he was inbound at ten thousand feet, descending, and making an instrument

Pat J. Macha at the PV-1 Bu No 49467 crash site on Hauser Mountain, circa 1999. *Photo by G.P. Macha.*

approach about ten miles from the airfield. Sadly, this was not the case, as 41-12363 was nowhere near Long Beach; it was, in fact, over the Mojave Desert, flying south toward the San Gabriel Mountain Range.

Ranchers and sheep herders near the small hamlets of Llano, Pearblossom and Valermo on the Mojave Desert reported hearing an aircraft flying in the clouds, its engines roaring as the pilot apparently realized that he was too low and flying into rugged mountainous terrain. The official USAAF accident report states that the pilot may have stalled the C-46A as he attempted to climb over the mountains at too steep an angle, causing the C-46A to slide backward. This tail-first slide caused the C-46 to crash, striking a large Jeffery Pine that stabbed the empennage and tail section like a sword, holding the wreckage high on the mountain while the fuselage, wings and engines plunged into a deep canyon on the northwest flank of 7,760-foot Pallett Mountain. All four men on board died instantly; their bodies, buried in deep snow, were not recovered until the late spring of 1944.

A Curtiss C-46A Commando 41-12363 tail assembly lanced on tree. Crash date March 20, 1944. Photo circa 1944. *Photo by Sewell F. Griggers.*

The author visited the C-46A crash site several times in the 1980s thanks to Los Angeles County ranger Jack Farley Jr. A flyover in 2010 showed that the tail was still lanced on the pine tree, but since then, the effects of gravity and the death of the tree due to numerous lightning strikes have caused the tail assembly to begin its inevitable slide into the canyon below. Faded yellow *X*s were still visible on the tail, wings and other parts of the Curtiss C-46A Commando, made famous during World War II for flying cargo from India over the Himalaya Mountains to China on a route known as "The Hump."

The Vultee BT-13 was the standard USAAF basic training aircraft during World War II. More than twenty BT-13 aircraft were destroyed in accidents in Los Angeles County during the war years. One of these was BT-13A 41-11444. Flown by Flight Officer Ray Schwartz Jr., age twenty-two, and Flight Officer Arthur S. Sears, age twenty, it had departed Victorville Army Air Field on the morning of June 26, 1944. The young pilots flew over the mountain community of Wrightwood in San Bernardino County before taking a westerly course along State Highway 2 into the Swarthout Valley, following its gradually rising canyon terrain that was rapidly narrowing.

The Curtiss C-46A 41-12363, with yellow *X* marking, showing the effects of weathering, circa 1989. *Photo by Pat J. Macha.*

Eyewitnesses saw the BT-13A flying only 300 feet above the roadway when the pilot suddenly tried to turn his plane around and fly back down the canyon. The BT-13A stalled and spun into the ground, instantly killing both flight officers. The training plane came down about 150 yards from the highway; it did not burn. The weather was clear, with calm winds, but density altitude was a factor. In thin mountain air, experienced pilots would not fly up canyons at 6,500 feet.

The Lockheed P-38 Lightning was a common sight over Los Angeles County during the war years. The twin-engine, twin-boomed fighter was one aircraft that most Angelenos could easily identify. The P-38 was manufactured at the Lockheed Plant at Burbank Airport, where more than five thousand examples were built. The P-38 was also the designated air defense interceptor should enemy aircraft appear over the county. P-38s were based at the Lomita Fighter Strip, now Torrance Airport's Zamperini Field. P-38s also flew from Van Nuys Airport and Oxnard Fighter Strip in Ventura County.

More than twenty-five P-38s crashed in the county during the war. One of these was P-38L 44-24918, flown on September 20, 1944, by Lockheed production test pilot Roy C. Cameron, a highly experienced civilian aviator. Mr.

Flight Officer Ray Schwartz Jr. was only twenty-two years old when he was killed in a training plane crash on June 26, 1944. *Courtesy Bill DeBolt.*

Cameron's flight assignment had been to thoroughly test the pilot's oxygen system at high altitude, and to that end, he had flown north from Burbank to an area near Bakersfield, where he reported at 2:28 p.m. that he was at 29,000 feet. He then asked for a radio check. No other communications were received from Mr. Cameron. The Los Angeles Basin was covered that afternoon by stratus clouds up to an altitude of 4,500 feet. At 3:33 p.m., radio test engineers working on 5,441-foot Mount Harvard in the San Gabriel Mountains, just south of Mount Wilson, reported seeing a P-38 flying just below the cloud layer and traveling at a high rate of speed when it collided with and exploded on 4,795-foot Mount Yale. The impact occurred on the west face of Mount Yale at 4,345 feet MSL.

The accident investigators were at a loss to explain the exact cause of the crash. Malfunction of the pilot's oxygen system was discussed, as were the possibilities of a medical problem that affected the pilot. The cause of Mr. Cameron's demise remains a mystery to this day. When the author visited the crash site in December 1995, much of the smashed Lightning fighter remained on site, including the pair of long-silent Allison V-1710-111 inline engines that each developed the 1,475 horsepower that propelled the P-38L to a maximum speed of 414 miles per hour.

Although unexplained tragedy strikes, so, too, does incredible good luck happen to aviators who are facing certain death. This was the case for the pilot and passenger of AAF Cessna UC-78 42-58362 en route from Lemoore

AAF in Kings County, California, to March AAF in Riverside County on October 6, 1944. The pilot of the UC-78 was an AAF second lieutenant with 523 hours of flight experience, and his passenger was an AAF technical sergeant. While flying over Los Angeles County on the last leg of his flight, the pilot elected to cross the San Gabriel Mountains, during which he experienced power failure, causing him to crash-land two thousand feet below a timbered ridgeline. Incredibly, the UC-78, also called the Bamboo Bomber because of its mostly wooden construction, came to rest in an area of dense manzanita plants, which cushioned the forces of the impact. The tech sergeant suffered no injuries, but the pilot did receive injuries to his face and head. Both men decided not to take shelter in their wrecked aircraft and instead hiked to the nearest ridge top, from which they could see State Highway 2, and hunkered down for the night. The next morning, they climbed down to the highway and walked to a nearby ranger station, where they were then driven into Los Angeles for medical attention.

The accident board determined that the pilot had approached the mountains at too low an altitude and that the failure of the engines was due to a fuel mismanagement issue. The pilot was held responsible for being the cause of the crash and was disciplined. The wreckage of the UC-78 was not recovered following the crash, and its fabric-covered frame remains today, minus its engines, which were taken out by helicopter in the 1970s. Somewhere in the upper reaches of Cooper Canyon, the UC-78 remains, overgrown, in a wild and unburned area of the Angeles National Forest. This is one wreck that the author has failed to find, but hopefully it will be noticed one day and conserved for the historic aircraft that it is. The UC-78 was made famous in the 1950s TV program *Sky King*.

During the course of World War II, half a dozen navy and marine aircraft crashed on or into the ocean near Santa Catalina and San Clemente Islands, with fatal results for more than twenty men. In one tragic case, a navy pilot ditched his fighter aircraft successfully but was unable to free himself from the cockpit before it sank in deep water east of Avalon. San Clemente Island is in Los Angeles County, but it is owned and operated by the U.S. Navy. Parts of this island and the waters around it were used as bombing and gunnery ranges before, during and after World War II. Castle Rock, just off the northwest tip of the island, was used extensively as a bombing and gunnery target, and several navy aircraft were lost during these activities.

Another notable accident at Catalina Island during World War II involved the loss of a U.S. Navy airship, a Goodyear K-series Blimp, assigned to an antisubmarine warfare patrol on October 17, 1944. Most K-series airships were powered by two Pratt & Whitney R-1340-AN-2 engines, which provide a top speed of seventy-five miles per hour. The K-series Blimps had crews of three officers and six enlisted ratings. The K-111 could be armed with four depth charges and one flex-mounted Browning .50-inch machine gun. The K-111 had a range of two thousand miles while cruising fully loaded at forty-six miles per hour.

The 10:00 p.m. departure of the K-111 on October 17, 1944, from the Naval Auxiliary Air Facility at Del Mar in San Diego County was to begin a twenty-two-hour operational training and patrol mission that would take the K-111 northwest to Newport Beach in Orange County and then on a course to the east end of Santa Catalina Island. From there, the K-111 was to fly south to a point near Scammon's Lagoon in Mexico's Baja California Del Norte and then fly back to Del Mar. Dense stratus clouds and fog obscured the Southern California coastline, and the K-111 flew farther north than intended until it finally turned and headed toward Catalina Island. Although the K-111 was radar equipped and the navigator could see the island on his scope, the pilot officer did not change his course. Instead, he ordered the second pilot to climb to 1,500 feet, but the K-111 struck a mountain ridgeline west of Avalon at 11:30 p.m., killing five crewmen and critically injuring three others, one of whom would die the following day. Two other crewmen received only minor injuries.

U.S. Navy K-series blimp, similar to the K-111 that crashed on Catalina Island in October 1944. *Courtesy American Aviation Historical Society.*

The K-111 had struck the island and burst into flames at 1,450 feet above sea level, southwest of Avalon, where the highest mountain is 1,684-foot East Peak. It is a miracle that anyone survived the inferno that burned more than two acres of rugged ground. Today, scant remnants of the K-111's crew cabin (or "car"), engine parts and some propeller blades still remain in a steep thicket recess on Santa Catalina Island.

In Wildcat Gulch, near Barley Flats on Highway 2, there occurred the crash of an AAF Douglas C-47B 43-16143 with a crew of two and eleven passengers on board. The crash happened during a blinding snowstorm on the night of November 11, 1944. The army transport had taken off from Hamilton AAF in Marin County via Bakersfield en route to Mines Field (LAX today) in Los Angeles County. The official AAF accident report stated that the pilot was given an inadequate weather briefing prior to departing Bakersfield. The pilot did know that instrument flight rules would be required, and radio communications were lost shortly after takeoff, impeding his ability to fly the prescribed course south along what is today Interstate 5. Instead, the C-47B was flown on a southeasterly heading when a powerful storm front that stretched across Southern California was encountered. The storm produced rain over the Los Angeles Basin and snowfall at higher elevations in the San Gabriel Mountains. Severe icing conditions prevailed along the flight path as well. The pilot, perhaps believing that he had cleared the mountains, began his descent too soon, resulting in a collision with trees on a mountain ridge and plunging the C-47B into Wildcat Gulch at 8:17 p.m.

The wrecked C-47B was not located until the afternoon of November 12, and the first rescue teams to arrive in the accident area were hampered by snowdrifts and darkness. The crash site was finally reached at 8:00 a.m. on November 13, and the recovery of the injured and dead could finally be accomplished.

The official accident report states that all on board died instantly, but this is not true. Based on the eyewitness account of Los Angeles County Sheriff's Department first responder Lieutenant Sewell F. Griggers, as well as subsequent newspaper articles, at least two passengers were transported to an area hospital alive and one other passenger died at the crash scene before he could be transported by the rescue teams.

The wreckage of the C-47B was partly removed by an aluminum salvager in the 1960s, but more than 30 percent of the aircraft was still visible when the author visited the crash site in September 1990. Fires have since burned in the crash area, but the widely scattered and unmarked wreckage is visible from the air, north of Barley Flats off Highway 2.

The loss of an Army Air Force Consolidated B-24J Liberator heavy bomber and its entire crew of ten men on December 22, 1944, is somewhat of a mystery. What began as a routine instrument training flight that departed Muroc Army Airfield in San Bernardino County at 8:00 a.m. ended in tragedy minutes after 6:11 p.m., when a B-24J crewman radioed Muroc indicating that they were lost and needed a vector. What happened is not known, but the following possible causes were listed in the official accident report: in-flight explosion or loss of control during pull up, causing the aircraft to disintegrate. The wreckage of the Liberator was scattered almost three thousand yards. It required about a week to locate all of the bodies of the crew due to rugged terrain and the high-altitude nature of the in-flight breakup. The wreckage was first seen from the air on November 23, 1944, by the pilot of an army search plane, and ground teams sent to the crash site hoped to find some B-24J crewmen alive who might have bailed out of their stricken aircraft. Unfortunately, this was not to be the case.

Two Army Vultee BT-13Bs were sent from Grand Central Airport to look for missing members of the B-24J crew on November 24. First Lieutenant Merle D. Armstrong was flying BT-13B 42-90434, but as he was circling the B-24J crash site, he flew too close to a ridgeline on Mount Gleason and crashed, miraculously suffering only minor injuries. His wingman in a second BT-13B radioed First Lieutenant Armstrong, and amazingly, Armstrong was able to reply that he was okay, even though his aircraft was destroyed! It was determined by the safety board that severe clear-air turbulence was a factor in the crash. Because of the inaccessible location, the wrecked BT-13B was abandoned by the army.

Yellow Xs were painted on the wings and tail to indicate that it was not a missing aircraft, and then it was largely forgotten until March 10, 1951, when a Cessna 140, flown by two members of the Civil Air Patrol (CAP), began circling the BT-13B and B-24J crash sites. The CAP men were on a training mission looking at old aircraft wrecks near the upper reaches of Big Tujunga Canyon and the Angeles Forest Highway in an area then known as the "graveyard of aircraft." The Cessna 140 crashed into the bottom of a steep canyon, killing both men on board, possibly due to the similar winds that had helped bring down the nearby wreck of the BT-13B. Not long after this tragic accident, most of the BT-13B wreckage was removed for its scrap value. Today, only the landing gear and a few other small parts remain on the crash site. The Cessna 140 has been mostly removed, too, but its crew—Master Sergeant Russell Fewell, pilot, and Private Peter Bessolo, observer—are remembered as the first Civil Air Patrol fatalities in Southern California.

One wreck (the B-24J) begets another (the BT-13B) and then another (the Cessna 140). This is the only double-accident scenario involving one existing crash site in Los Angeles County that the author is aware of. In 1966, when the author visited the B-24J crash site in the Middle Fork of Mill Creek, southeast of Mount Gleason, it exhibited no fire damage except at main impact above the creek bed. Years of intermittent heavy rains and floods have buried most of the B-24J under rocks and debris.

A total of three B-24s crashed in the county during World War II, all in 1944, killing a total of twenty-three airmen. Lockheed P-38 losses in 1944 totaled twelve, in which nine pilots were killed. Vultee BT-13 basic trainers accounted for nine losses with two fatalities. The year 1945 would see a dramatic reduction in military aviation accidents as the training and other operational activities declined, but fatal accidents would not abate entirely.

Airlines played an important role during World War II, transporting civilians and military personnel traveling on defense-related business or home on leave. Our military men and women had priority regarding seating, and sometimes civilians were bumped from their scheduled flights when necessary to ensure continuity in the war effort. Such was the case for Hollywood actress Donna Reed, who had planned to fly on American Air Lines Flight 6001 from El Paso, Texas, to Burbank Airport on January 10, 1945. As Miss Reed was about to board AAL Douglas DC-3 NC-25684, she was asked to surrender her seat, and she gladly did so, to an army officer with business in the Los Angeles area. In fact, all of the passengers on board were military men, including four serving in the navy and seventeen serving in the army. Flight 6001 departed for Burbank at about 1:45 a.m. local time, with the DC-3 cruising at 165 miles per hour, and arrived in the Burbank area at 4:06 a.m. It was seen flying across the airport perimeter just under the stratus cloud base and then turning in an easterly direction. Witnesses at the field said that the landing gear was retracted and that the landing lights were off. Moments later, the pilot radioed Burbank Tower that he could no longer see the airport and that he was diverting to Palmdale due to the low clouds and fog that obscured his approach. The pilot also mentioned problems with his radio reception at 4:07 p.m. Burbank Tower acknowledged his message and asked him to contact the air traffic control (ATC) center for clearance to Palmdale, but no further messages were received from the airliner.

At 9:30 a.m., as the fog and clouds dissipated, men in the Burbank control tower spotted the smoldering wreckage of American Air Lines Flight 6001 almost three miles northeast of the field in the Verdugo Mountains. All twenty-one passengers and three crew members perished in the crash; a

American Air Lines Douglas DC-3, similar to one lost on January 10, 1945, in the Verdugo Mountains. *Courtesy William T. Larkins.*

post-impact fire had consumed the fuselage and center section of the DC-3. Only the tail assembly and the outer wing panels remained intact. The crash site was located between rugged McClure and Brace Canyons at 1,650 feet MSL. Once the grim task of recovering the remains of those on board had been completed, salvage of the remaining aircraft structure was undertaken, and the Civil Aeronautics Board (CAB) began the long process of determining the cause of the accident. The board's findings were made public on September 24, 1945: "[A]fter making a standard instrument let-down approach the pilot elected to make a missed approach procedure, but in doing so failed to modify the procedure by flying away from the hills, instead he flew towards them." The board also stated that "the pilot had not been properly advised of the latest weather conditions at Burbank," calling it "negligence on the part of airline personnel, for not having radioed the updated information."

The accident scene of Flight 6001 is seldom visited today; remaining debris is less than 5 percent of the original aircraft. Chaparral covers the place where twenty-four people lost their lives not to a major storm front but rather, in part, to the low clouds and fog that are still common in Los Angeles Basin.

January 17, 1945, was cold and clear when a flight of four Lockheed P-38J fighters flying from Van Nuys Army Air Field approached an area near 5,481-foot-high Black Butte on the Mojave Desert. The area around the butte was often used for combat tactics training. P-38J 42-103986, piloted by

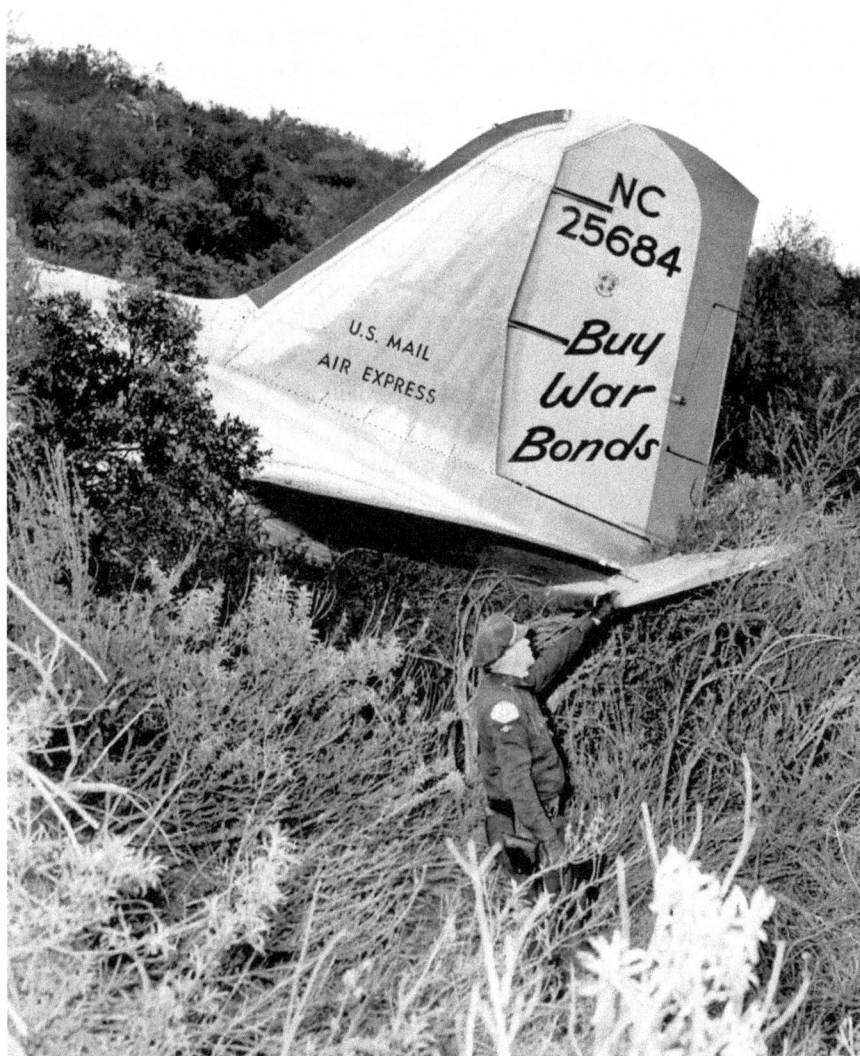

Tail assembly of the wrecked American Air Lines Douglas DC-3 NC-25684 in the Verdugo Mountains. *Courtesy D.D. Hatfield Collection.*

twenty-six-year-old Second Lieutenant Robert J. Sleske, started its descent to the desert below at 10,000 feet, achieving a high rate of speed in the process and perhaps causing the young lieutenant to black out as he attempted to recover from the dive. At 10:40 a.m., 42-103986 struck the desert floor just east of Black Butte, disintegrating and killing Second Lieutenant Sleske instantly. The wreckage of the P-38J was scattered over one quarter mile, yet few parts of the aircraft burned because the high-speed impact caused the fuel to vaporize, producing a flash explosion only. A small memorial of piled rocks and P-38 parts, along with an American flag, now mark the site.

Second Lieutenant Sleske would not be the only P-38 fatality on January 17. Another flight of four P-38s, also flying from Van Nuys Army Air Field, were engaged in combat tactics training about thirty-five miles northwest of Black Butte flying over the Antelope Valley. Second Lieutenant Austin G. Strickland was at the controls of Lockheed P-38J 44-23421 flying at thirteen thousand feet, where he was to have performed aerobatic maneuvers, but the flight leader saw Second Lieutenant Strickland's P-38J descending in a flat spin that would have precluded pilot bailout due to centrifugal forces pinning a pilot in his seat or blacking him out. The P-38J struck the flat desert floor at 12:50 p.m., remaining remarkably intact. The gravity loads, however, killed Second Lieutenant Strickland instantly. No trace of this crash remains today on lands once used by barley farmers.

The jet age began during World War II in the United States with the development of the first turbo-jet fighter for the U.S. Army Air Force by the Bell Aircraft Corporation. The Bell design was designated P-59 Airacomet, and it was powered by two General Electric I-18 turbo jet engines. The armament was impressive, with one 37mm cannon and three .50-inch machine guns. The overall performance of P-59 caused the type to be relegated to test or training units. One of these units was the 29th Fighter Squadron, assigned to the 412th Fighter Group, based at Palmdale Army Air Field.

On March 1, 1945, two Bell P-59A fighters departed Palmdale AAF at 9:00 a.m., assigned to fly low-level circuits near antiaircraft gun positions so the gunners could practice tracking jet targets. Germany already had an operational jet fighter, the Messerschmitt 262, and this type of antiaircraft training was considered imperative. At 9:20 a.m., P-59A 44-22626, flown by Second Lieutenant Howard L. Wilson, was flying toward P-59A 44-22620, flown by Second Lieutenant Robert W. Murdock at five hundred feet above ground level (AGL), when they collided almost head on. Both Airacomets caromed through the air, shedding parts and crashing, killing both pilots. The estimated speed at the time of impact was 350 miles per hour. After nearly seventy years, parts of the ill-fated P-59s lie scattered across the desert southeast of Black Butte near the San Bernardino County Line.

Navy and marine pilots were not immune from accidents, either. On March 19, 1945, a navy Grumman FM-2 Wildcat caught fire in-flight east of the Newhall Pass, but the pilot successfully bailed out without injury. The navy lost a Grumman TBM Avenger on April 6, 1945, killing the three-man crew when it flew into the Palos Verdes Hills that border the Catalina Channel. Dense coastal fog was a factor in this accident.

An evening navigational training flight of four Lockheed P-38s based at Van Nuys Army Air Field went terribly wrong about one hour into the mission on April 19, 1945. A U.S. Army Air Force second lieutenant, age twenty-two, was to perform high-altitude aerobatics at twenty-one thousand feet; he started a series of required maneuvers, but P-38L 44-25300 went to a steep dive. As the pilot attempted to recover, parts were seen falling off his aircraft. The pilot then attempted to bail out, but he struck the horizontal stabilizer, severing his left leg at the hip. Both the P-38L and its pilot plunged onto Sierra Pelona Ridge. Prior to impact, the P-38L tail assembly completely separated from aircraft, coming down nearly a mile from where the wings, engines and cockpit landed. The pilot's body was found six hundred feet from this main impact zone. World War II combat flying was always dangerous, but operational training could be hazardous too.

August 19, 1945, was a clear-weather day, perfect for four naval aviators who departed Los Alamitos Naval Auxiliary Air Station to practice combat tactics over Santa Catalina Island in their Vought Corsair fighters. Their training regimen included a series of mock dogfights that required the pilots to use every technique they had learned, including the famous Thatch Weave. Somehow, shortly after 2:00 p.m., a collision occurred that tore the massive two-thousand-horsepower R-2800 engine from F4U-1D Bu No 57879, sending it into an upside-down flat spin. The pilot, Ensign Joseph W. Mapes, managed to bail out, but he struck the horizontal stabilizer of his F4U-1D, breaking both of his legs. One of his two fractures was a compound, causing Ensign Mapes to suffer great pain as he landed near the edge of a cliff overlooking the ocean. His spinning Corsair landed upside down almost intact in a canyon nearby, while its engine plunged into the sea. Ensign Robert B. Frackler successfully parachuted from his stricken Goodyear-built FG-1 Corsair Bu No 13559, and he landed on the face of cliff, where he was rescued by two men with ropes, enabling the young ensign to climb to safety. Ensign Frackler sustained burns to his arms, along with numerous cuts and bruises. His FG-1 broke up and sank as it hit the Pacific Ocean southwest of the island. The cause of the midair collision was attributed to the flight leader for turning into the sun, causing the pilots to lose sight of each other.

The author visited the wreck of Ensign Mapes's Corsair in 1988 and was amazed at what was seen. Remote and undisturbed, the Vought-built F4U-1D Bu No 57879 wreck is now a part of Catalina's World War II history.

The upside-down and unburned wreck of U.S. Navy Vought F4U-1D Bu No 57879 Corsair on Catalina Island. Crash date August 19, 1945. *Courtesy Kirk McKewon.*

On September 21, 1945, First Lieutenant Walter W. Dirrim was posted missing on a short flight from Burbank Airport to Palmdale AAF. The weather between the two fields was enshrouded in dense stratus clouds at the time of the flight. The aircraft type involved was a North American Aviation AT-6D "Texan" advanced trainer, serial number 44-81618, assigned to Muroc AAF. The wreckage of the missing plane was located late the next day atop Sierra Pelona Ridge, and the body of First Lieutenant Dirrim was recovered on September 23, 1945. The army accident report stated that the pilot had tried to fly under the clouds (scud running) and then tried to fly over a ridge instead of around it. The Sierra Pelona Ridge and its highest point, 5,187-foot Mount McDill, have proven to be a dangerous area for pilots to navigate when weather conditions require the use of instrument flight rules (IFR) and not visual flight rules (VFR).

The weather on September 21, 1945, was a factor in the fatal loss of Lieutenant Commander Richard H. Procter, a U.S. Navy Reserve officer, who departed Mines Field (LAX) en route to Palm Springs. Lieutenant Commander Procter was flying the navy version of the famed NAA

T-6 Texan trainer known as the SNJ. When SNJ-6 Bu No 112349 was posted missing late on September 21, a search effort was launched, and the wreckage was located on 5,409-foot Monrovia Peak on September 23. Los Angeles County sheriff Lieutenant Sewell F. Griggers led the recovery effort on September 24, 1945, to the crash site of the SNJ-6, which was located at the 4,700-foot level of the rugged peak in the San Gabriel Mountains. World War II had formally ended on September 2, 1945, but the sacrifices of our military personnel would continue. Today, the wreckage of the SNJ-6 lies in a steep canyon, where it was pushed to make it less visible from the burgeoning population in Los Angeles Basin below.

Two U.S. Navy Lockheed PV-1 Ventura patrol bombers collided over the Pacific Ocean on September 26, 1945, destroying both aircraft and killing six crewmen aboard Bu No 34921, flown by Lieutenant Junior Grade Willard J. Smith. PV-1 Bu No 34738, flown by Ensign Walter Wright, USNR, was successfully ditched, with all six crewmen escaping before the Ventura sank in deep water, though not without moderate to serious injuries sustained by all on board. The accident occurred while flying in formation five miles southwest of Catalina Island.

In the last months of 1945, the final aviation accidents occured, starting with a USAAF transport aircraft, a Curtiss C-46A Commando 41-5190. On October 2, 1945, the C-46A departed Ontario Army Air Field at 1:00 a.m. en route to Reno Army Air Field in Nevada. The Commando was manned by a crew of three and included one passenger, a Women's Army Corps nurse, Lieutenant Martha S. Betts. For unknown reasons, the pilot chose a flight path that took the massive cargo craft over the San Gabriel Mountains, west of his stated flight path, over 4,190-foot Cajon Pass. Instead, the C-46A was flying northwesterly near the highest peak, Mount San Antonio, also known as Mount Baldy, towering 10,068 feet, which straddles the Los Angeles and San Bernardino County lines. The starboard wing of the C-46A struck the south slope of Mount Baldy at 1:15 a.m. only 300 feet below the crest in San Bernardino County, careening into the saddle between east and west Baldy before plunging over the north side, leaving a trail of debris and death behind. The majority of the wreckage was scattered into Los Angeles County, where it can be seen today from Highway 2, shining like a diamond from late spring to early fall when the sun's rays are just right. The place to see the shine is from the parking lot at the Lightning Ridge Nature Trail.

October 29 ended the year 1945 with a fatal accident near Acton on the southwest side of Highway 14 near Kentucky Springs. Another crew

Left: Pat J. Macha with a propeller blade from the USAAF Curtiss C-46A 41-5190, which crashed on Mount San Antonio on October 2, 1945, killing three crewmen and one passenger. *Photo by Chris LeFave.*

Below: Grumman TBM-3 Avenger, similar to the one lost on October 29, 1945, in the Soledad Pass near Acton. *Courtesy William T. Larkins.*

was flying in dense clouds and fog en route from Goleta Marine Corps Air Station (MCAS) in Santa Barbara County to Mojave Marine Corps Air Station in Kern County via the Soledad Pass.

The Grumman TBM-3E Bu No 69190 was assigned to Service Squadron MASG-51 and was piloted by Second Lieutenant Leonard W. Carlson, USMCR. His mission was to deliver the mail and three passengers—Warrant Officer Walter R. Towers, USMC; Technical Sergeant Ray V. Stauffer, USMC; and Corporal Homer M. Barnes—to Mojave MCAS.

The crash occurred at 2:10 p.m. and was heard as a loud explosion by local residents. All on board the Grumman Avenger were killed instantly, and the crash touched off a small brush fire that was quickly contained. Some wreckage still remains scattered on two ridges and in the bottom of one small draw, where time stopped for four marines whose sad passing ends this chapter but not the continuing dangers of scud running.

CHAPTER 3

SKY'S THE LIMIT!

The end of World War II heralded a new age in aviation for Los Angeles County. Not only was the United States of America the most powerful nation militarily, but it was also the hands-down leader in the world of technology. The Southern California aviation industry was on the cutting edge of new military and commercial aircraft designs and manufacturing. New airliner production to meet the increasing demand for long-range, comfortable and faster aircraft was ramping up at Douglas and Lockheed, along with postwar automobile production. So, too, was the production of inexpensive and versatile light aircraft for use by the postwar public that included thousands of former servicemen and servicewomen who wanted to continue flying on a recreational or business basis.

On September 18, 1947, the United States Air Force was established as a separate branch of the armed services, and some of the World War II–era training fields in Los Angeles County were closed, while bases such as Van Nuys welcomed private, light and corporate aircraft. A California Air National Guard (ANG) contingent remained active at Van Nuys until 1990. In the 1950s, Palmdale Army Air Base (AAB) became Air Force Plant 42, where final assembly and testing of primarily military aircraft continues to take place. Daugherty Field in Long Beach continued to be a manufacturing center for the Douglas Aircraft Company (Boeing today), the navy auxiliary air station moved its operations to a new base in Orange County and the World War II army facility became an air guard base lasting into the late 1960s. Grand Central Airport closed in 1959, but Brackett Field, located in the eastern part of the county, was developed into a first-rate airport designed to accommodate a wide range of private and corporate aircraft. The Lomita Fighter Strip became Torrance Airport (Zamperini Field). Compton, San Fernando, El Monte and Whiteman Airport along Clover Field welcomed a host of small private aircraft. Jack Northrop Field became Hawthorne Municipal Airport, sharing its space with Northrop Aircraft Company. When Convair decided to sell Vultee Field in Downey following World War II, North American Aviation bought it and continued to manufacture there, finally closing the airfield in late 1956. With the Space Shuttle Program shutting down in 1998, the Downey facility closed for good in 1999.

Howard Hughes built a private airfield in 1941 at his Culver City manufacturing plant. When the runway was lengthened in the 1950s and paved, it became one of the world's longest privately owned paved airports, at 9,600 feet, until it closed in 1985.

There were relatively few aircraft accidents in 1946, but 1947 got off to rough start with the loss of twelve aircraft; many of these involved World War II surplus planes purchased for a fraction of their original cost from the War Assets Administration. The first major loss occurred on March 18, 1947, when a war surplus Beechcraft C-45 twin-engine light transport became lost in the fog after taking off from Burbank Airport and crashed in the Verdugo Mountains, with fatal results for both men on board. The landing gear, parts of wing and fuselage structures from the C-45 are still visible today above Brand Park. Fog and low clouds were factors in the loss of another war surplus aircraft on April 19, 1947, when a Cessna UC-78 Bobcat flew into the low hills while trying to fly out of the fog-enshrouded San Fernando Valley, killing all four persons on board.

The following day, Naval Reserve ensign T.B. Jones and his passenger, Pharmacist Mate First Class John O. Zimmerman, were flying from Los Alamitos Naval Reserve Air Station in Orange County on a routine training flight when increasing stratus clouds began to restrict the pilot's ability to navigate. The aircraft was the rugged and dependable North American Aviation SNJ-5 Bu No 52009. At 11:05 a.m. on April 20, 1947, the SNJ-5 plowed into a chaparral-covered ridge four miles north of the city of Glendora in the San Gabriel Mountains. The pilot, lost in the clouds, had just initiated a climb when he collided with undergrowth so dense that the aircraft traveled only thirty feet before coming to a stop. Neither man was injured, except for some bumps and bruises. As John Zimmerman told the author in a 2001 interview, they survived the crash "thanks to dumb luck." It took Jones and Zimmerman three and a half hours to hike down to the

San Dimas Forest Service Station. The ranger on duty added a red pin to his map, marking the approximate location of the SNJ-5. Zimmerman said there were already one hundred plane crash pins on the map. John Zimmerman told the ranger that the altimeter in the SNJ-5 was reading 3,800 feet MSL following the crash. The author and his son have spent some time trying to locate the wreckage of Bu No 52009, but to no avail.

On May 8, 1947, the pilot of a Piper Cub NC-88642 crashed in the fog near Zimmerman's SNJ-5, and he, too, walked away unscathed. One more pilot had some good luck in the fog when he crashed his single-seat biplane near the top of Beverly Glen at Mulholland Drive in the Santa Monica Mountains, escaping with only minor injuries.

July 2, 1947, dawned bright and clear when an army air force AT-6C Texan trainer, 42-48918, departed Long Beach Army Airfield at 10:00 a.m. for a local proficiency flight, with a return expected not later than noon. Lieutenant Edward F. Bickford was flying alone and apparently decided to fly over his home in the Pasadena area, where he engaged in aerobatic maneuvers, performing an aerial salute to his wife and child. Moments later, he was seen flying north, up a steep canyon, and crashed to his death below the ruins of the old Mount Lowe Resort. A column of smoke rose from the crash site, and the post-impact fire burned more than ten acres.

Los Angeles County sheriff's captain Sewell Griggers was first to see the wrecked AT-6C from the air and reported its location. The body of Lieutenant Edward F. Bickford was recovered the following day, and the wreckage was left in situ, as the terrain made it too difficult to remove. Lieutenant Bickford had served with distinction during World War II in Europe, where he was assigned to the 356th Fighter Squadron, flying sixty-eight combat missions in the P-51D Mustang. Lieutenant Bickford achieved "Ace" status with 5.5 confirmed kills, and later, for heroism during one ground attack mission, he earned the Distinguished Flying Cross and the Air Medal with four Oak Leaf Clusters. His squadron received a Presidential Unit Citation during the young lieutenant's combat tenure. Lieutenant Bickford remained in the U.S. Air Force Reserve (USAFR) following the war and completed his first year at the California Institute of Technology (Caltech). He was twenty-three years old at the time of his death, and his tragic passing left behind a young wife and a one-year-old daughter. Now in her late sixties, his daughter is still trying to understand what exactly happened on that July day that changed her life, and that of her mother, forever.

The company Fairchild Aerial Surveys was able to obtain a war surplus Douglas A-26C Invader light bomber, NC-37493. Famed for its speed and

Left: Lieutenant Edward F. Bickford was a highly decorated World War II fighter "Ace" with the Ninth Air Force in England. He lost his life on July 2, 1947, in the crash of an army AT-6C. *Courtesy Eileen Vesely.*

Below: Burned tail assembly of the Douglas A-26 NC-37493, which crashed in the Verdugo Mountains on August 25, 1947. *Courtesy D.D. Hatfield Collection.*

firepower during the final two years of World War II in Europe, the sleek twin-engine craft was to be used for aerial mapping assignments in South America when it departed Burbank Airport on the morning of August 25, 1947. The weather at the time of departure included the all-too-common low clouds and fog that obscured the nearby Verdugo Mountains. Just minutes after takeoff, the A-26 slammed into a ridge above Deer Canyon at 1,800 feet MSL, killing the highly experienced forty-year-old pilot, his thirty-eight-year-old wife and his mechanic, age twenty-five. Scattered wreckage from the A-26C can still be seen today on the steep and rugged slopes of the Verdugo Mountains.

Post–World War II protocols for flights involving prototype aircraft always included at least one chase aircraft for a number of reasons: safety, providing feedback to the flight test crew and documenting the test flight with both still images and motion picture video. These photos and films would be reviewed and evaluated in post-flight debriefings. Both military and civilian photographers were used to complete the photo documentation mission.

The Northrop Aircraft Corporation had one of the most experienced and longest-serving photographers and cameramen in the aerospace business. His name was Roy L. Wolford, and he worked for Northrop from the 1930s to the 1980s. Roy worked on the ground and in the air as the supervisor of engineering photography. His images are valued primary source material for aerospace historians and aficionados.

On October 21, 1947, Roy Wolford was assigned to fly a chase mission to photo document the Northrop YB-49 flying wing during a lengthy test flight over the Mojave Desert. Roy and one other photographer were flying in a Northrop P-61C 42-8322. The P-61C was a famous night fighter called the "Black Widow" during World War II. It was being flown by Northrop test pilot A.J. "Slim" Perrett, well known for not wearing his parachute, choosing instead to sit on it as a cushion. Roy and the other photographer were wearing their chutes—a good thing, too. As the P-61C flew beneath the YB-49 to film the extension and retraction of its landing gear, another chase aircraft, an air force Lockheed P-80A, called the crew of the P-61C to relate that its right engine was on fire, urging the crew to bail out. With smoke and flames beginning to spread across the right wing of the Black Widow, a bailout was ordered, with one crewmember bailing out immediately. Roy Wolford wanted to jump, too, but he stayed with the burning aircraft to help "Slim" Perrett put on his parachute on. Once that was accomplished, and with only moments to spare, Roy departed the cockpit, rolled out across the burning wing without catching fire and pulled his D-ring that allowed his

The Northrop P-61C used by the Northrop Aircraft Corporation as a photo platform during test flights of the YB-49 flying wing. *Courtesy William T. Larkins.*

parachute to deploy. Perrett was lucky, too; just as he stood up in an effort to bail out, the P-61C broke up, catapulting the pilot clear of two spinning propellers and the burning mass of metal that had been his aircraft. As the three crewmen floated earthward, the P-61C spun downward in an inverted position, hitting the desert floor and creating a thunderous explosion.

The cause of the P-61C loss was a ruptured fuel line, which allowed the high-octane aviation gasoline to reach the exhaust system on the starboard, or right, engine. Injuries were minor, with Mr. Perrett suffering abrasions in a sensitive area because he did not have enough time to properly buckle up his parachute harness. He swore that he'd always wear his parachute in the future, but he was killed test-flying a Northrop design called the Pioneer a short time later. A.J. "Slim" Perrett was unable to bail out of the Pioneer because the aircraft was flying too low at the time the emergency occurred for his parachute to be effective. The YB-49 that Roy Wolford had been filming at the time of the P-61C loss crashed on June 5, 1948, northwest of Muroc Air Force Base (AFB). All five crewmen on board the YB-49, including the pilot, Captain Glen W. Edwards, were killed. Muroc AFB was renamed Edwards AFB in honor of Captain Edwards.

The author visited the P-61C crash site in 2000 and again in 2001. The second visit was prompted by Roy Wolford's request for a few small parts of the aircraft he had flown in on so many air-to-air photo missions prior to that fateful day in October 1947. Roy met with the author in 2001 at the Western Museum of Flight, where he told his story of helping to save another man's

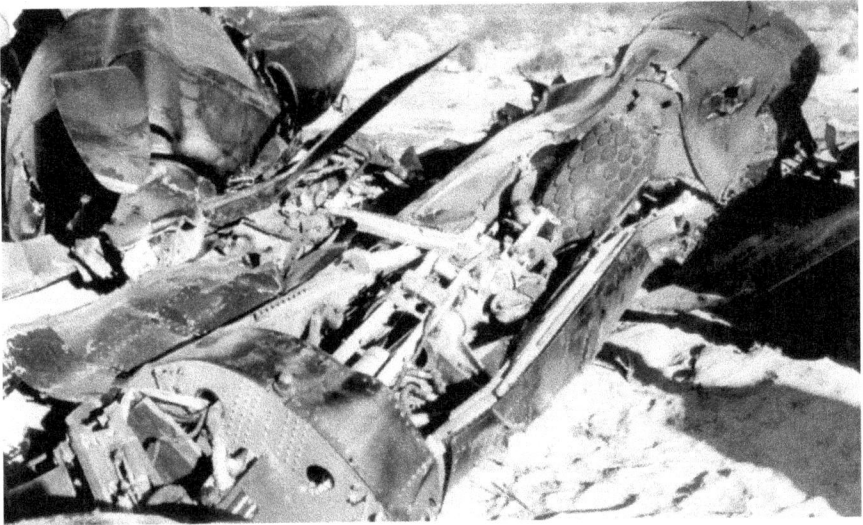

The Northrop P-61C 42-8322, upside-down on the Mojave Desert, with the left engine and bent propeller blades astride the fuselage and the nose landing gear retracted. *Courtesy Roy L. Wolford.*

life at great risk to his own. Roy passed away in February 2013, a legendary figure in the annals of Northrop Aircraft Company's history. The P-61C wreckage is still visible east of Palmdale near a scattered collection of small homes, but sadly, it has become a dumpsite today for all types of trash.

Test flights over the Antelope Valley usually originated from Muroc AFB on the Mojave Desert. Muroc was renamed Edwards AFB in December 1949. Today, it is officially known as the Air Force Flight Test Center (AFFTC). Test pilots often came from the ranks of World War II–era fighter pilots with proven flying abilities and "Ace" statuses. One such pilot was First Lieutenant Robert A. Hoover, assigned to the P-84B Thunderjet flight test program. The Thunderjet was built by Republic Aviation in Farmingdale, Long Island, New York. A straight-wing design with a single Allison J-35 turbojet engine, and armed with six .50-inch machine guns, it could reach speeds up to six hundred miles per hour.

On November 26, 1947, First Lieutenant Hoover was following a specified flight plan during which the J-35 made a loud noise and began to vibrate widely. A fire warning light came on, and the young officer jettisoned his wing tip fuel tanks and started a long glide back to Muroc. Hoover then noticed a trail of black smoke following his aircraft, followed by smoke in the cockpit and oil spraying on his windscreen. At this point, Hoover elected to bail out; as the early jets lacked ejection seats, he crawled over the side and let go. Unfortunately, he struck the horizontal stabilizer, breaking one leg. Hoover was unconscious for a few moments and then came to just in time to pull the D-ring and open his parachute before making a rough landing, being dragged for nearly one hundred feet. Local residents drove First Lieutenant Hoover to the hospital in Lancaster. The P-84B had come down near the Los Angeles Aqueduct and Highway 138.

Most of the wreckage was removed by the air force, and the site was forgotten until the author found it quite by chance when visiting friends who live at Three Points in the Western Antelope Valley. Wanting to show the property they had just purchased, the group drove across Highway 138, crossing the Los Angeles Aqueduct, and the author remembered photos in the air force accident report depicting a section of straight road on flat desert. The driver stopped, and the author walked out one hundred feet on open ground and found the micro site remains of P-84B 45-59502. Small parts littered the ground, some with the Republic Aviation prefix numbers 30- and 38-, confirming that the author had found the Thunderjet once piloted by First Lieutenant R.A. "Bob" Hoover.

First Lieutenant Hoover recovered from his injuries and continued his flight test career with North American Aviation at LAX. He flew the F-86 Sabre Jet and the F-100 Super Sabre. On July 7, 1955, Bob Hoover was forced to eject from an F-100A 52-5757 when he was unable to recover from a flat spin. The crash site is located south of Alpine Buttes in the Antelope Valley, where the author visited the remnants of the 52-5757 in 2002. Bob Hoover has been described as one of the finest test and demonstration pilots in the world. He called Los Angeles County home for most of his fine career.

San Clemente Island, located some forty-one miles off the California coast, continues to be used by the navy for bombing and gunnery practice, as well as for Seal Team training. On the morning of February 7, 1948, a navy Grumman TBM-3E Avenger was engaged in glide bombing practice over the island when it crashed, killing both crewmen. The exact cause of the accident has never been determined, but two possibilities are suspected, according to the findings of naval investigators: premature detonation of a bomb as it was being released from the bomb bay or structural failure due to the high G loads experienced during pullout. The investigators also found that the second crewman on board may have been able to bail out had he not been in the gun turret. The scattered wreckage of TBM-3E Bu No 86061 is visible near the south end of San Clemente Island on Google Earth.

While the fates can be cruel, luck can be kind as well, as James A. Meek, pilot of a World War II surplus light transport plane, and his mechanic, Gordon A. LaFord, found out on May 7, 1948. The two were flying from Culver City Airport to Tulare Airport in Tulare County, California, at night when they flew into the dense stratus clouds obscuring the San Gabriel Mountains. Looming out of the darkness were tall trees and steep canyon walls, a terrifying sight for the two men to behold. Switching on his landing light, the pilot throttled back on the six-hundred-horsepower Pratt & Whitney R-1340 engine as he lowered his flaps to slow the Noorduyn Norseman NC-54231, which was now flying just above stall speed. Seconds later, the pilot chopped the throttle completely, and his plane crashed through thickets of scrub plants and small trees, stopping in a saddle above the Saucer Branch at 3,200 feet MSL. West of the crash site was 4,466-foot Brown Mountain, and east of the wreck was a ridgeline leading to Lowe, Markham and San Gabriel peaks. Both men sustained severe contusions and abrasions, but they were able to walk, so they spent the night working their way down to the Sunset Ridge Ranger Station, where they were immediately transported to a hospital for treatment.

The Norseman aircraft that Mr. Meek was flying had been built in Canada for use as an eight- to ten-seat utility transport, designed to withstand the rigors of terrain and climate anywhere on earth. During World War II, the army air force purchased 746 Norseman, designated UC-64A. The UC-64A could operate with wheels or floats and became famous

The Canadian-built Noorduyn Norseman, similar to one lost in a nonfatal crash on May 7, 1948. *Courtesy William T. Larkins.*

Brothers Herb, Don and Bob Lank hold an aileron from the 1948 wreck of Noorduyn Norseman NC-54231, circa 1968. *Photo by G.P. Macha.*

as the aircraft type when renowned band leader Glenn Miller disappeared while flying in a UC-64A over the English Channel on December 15, 1944.

The author first visited Mr. Meek's Norseman crash site in 1966 and again in 1968. Both hikes involved a perilous crossing on an old pipeline attached by cables to a sheer rock wall below the Saucer Branch. The pipeline is gone today, but the author's son discovered another, albeit longer route to the Norseman site in April 1995. Because the UC-64A was a fabric-covered aircraft, it is virtually invisible today, as the fabric has disintegrated with the passage of time. The main spar was made of wood and can still be seen with metal wing ribs attached.

In the years following the Norseman accident, some salvage work was done by Jim Kofahl, a man who supplemented his income by removing useable parts from old wrecks; he would remove aircraft aluminum to sell for the going price per pound. Mr. Kofahl was a pilot himself, and he knew the salvage trade well. His work in the salvage field spanned nearly forty years, ending in the 1980s. He removed the landing gear from the Norseman, along with the instruments and some other small parts, too. In the 1970s and early 1980s, the author interviewed Mr. Kofahl several times about his work. The great rainstorms of 1969 and 1982 have ravaged the Norseman crash site, but most of the now-mangled wreckage is still there, scattered along the upper reaches of the Saucer Branch where, long ago, two men were so very lucky.

While accidents happen for many reasons, weather factors, mechanical failures and human factors can be part of the story too. From 1947 to 1949,

Amphibian Air Transport Inc. operated three Sikorsky S-43 twin-engine, high-wing, twenty-two-passenger amphibious aircraft for the route between Long Beach and Avalon on Santa Catalina Island. Early on the morning of September 4, 1948, a company pilot was assigned to fly the empty S-43 from Avalon back to Long Beach, but he crashed during his attempted takeoff. The pilot had been scheduled to depart from the floating seaplane base at Hamilton Cove by 8:00 a.m. with his copilot, but unbeknownst to anyone, he had been drinking heavily that night. The pilot made an unauthorized solo takeoff in dense fog at 3:20 a.m., but he did not fly far, crashing into the rocks two miles north of Avalon near the mouth of Rattlesnake Canyon. The S-43 sustained major damage, and first responders thought that the pilot was probably deceased; to their surprise, they found him alive. The pilot was transported to Avalon Hospital in serious condition, and he was later moved to a hospital in Long Beach. The thirty-six-year-old recovered from his injuries to face ensuing legal troubles. Most of the wrecked Sikorsky was recovered within a week of the accident, but some parts of the S-43 have been reported by divers in recent years on the ocean bottom just off the rocks north of Hamilton Cove.

The year 1949 marked an increase in scheduled airline traffic, and non-scheduled airlines were also beginning to appear at this time, offering lower

The Sikorsky S-43 amphibian wrecked north of Hamilton Cove on September 4, 1948. *Courtesy D.D. Hatfield Collection.*

The Curtiss C-46F N79978, of New Standard Airlines, which crashed on Chatsworth Peak on July 12, 1949. *Courtesy William T. Larkins.*

fares and more competition for the major air carriers. The non-scheduled air carriers used war surplus cargo and transport aircraft converted to comfortable passenger airliners. The Curtiss C-46 Commando was a non-scheduled favorite because of its range and seating capacity.

New Standard Airlines was one of the non-scheduled carriers that operated flights into and out of the Los Angeles metropolitan area. On July 12, 1949, Curtiss C-46F N79978, flight number 897R, crashed and burned on 2,314-foot Chatsworth Peak west of the San Fernando Valley, killing thirty-five passengers and crew. Miraculously, twelve passengers and one flight attendant survived, all with serious injuries, as they escaped the post-impact fire with only a few moments to spare.

Flight 897R originated in New York on July 11 and proceeded to Southern California, with stops at Chicago, Kansas City and Albuquerque and with Burbank Airport being the final destination. On the morning of July 12, as the C-46F approached Burbank, stratus clouds blanketed the Los Angeles Basin, and air traffic control required the pilot to fly five hundred feet above the cloud tops until the signal to land was given. At 7:36 a.m., Flight 897R was given clearance to make a straight in approach to land at Burbank; the pilot acknowledged, and that was the last transmission received. Moments later, the C-46F crashed into Chatsworth Peak in the Simi Hills.

The CAB found that the pilot had descended below prescribed minimum altitude while starting his turn back toward Burbank Airport, and in doing so, he was at fault, causing a fatal accident that was entirely avoidable. The wreckage was removed, but small parts of the C-46F and personal effects were reported at the site as late as 1995. Dishware and other items from the galley of N79978 were found around this time, too. Non-scheduled airlines would continue to operate for only a few more years as a result of more federal regulation and a slightly higher accident rate.

The stratus clouds that were a factor in the loss of the New Standard Airlines C-46F on July 11 would again be a factor in the loss of a U.S. Navy Douglas R4D-6 Bu No 17279 on July 13, 1949. The R4D-6 is the navy version of the air force's C-47, C-53 and the commercial DC-3. Bu No 17279 had departed Moffett Field in the San Francisco Bay area en route to Clover Field (Santa Monica Airport). The R4D-6 carried a crew of two and five passengers; flying under instrument flight rules, they were directed by Los Angeles Municipal Airport (LAX) to Clover Field, but the pilot seemed off course as he flew over Santa Monica. He asked if there were any obstructions ahead, and he received an emphatic answer: yes! There were obstructions: the Santa Monica Mountains. Tragically, it was too late, and the R4D-6 crashed into Dry Canyon, where it exploded and burned just three hundred feet below the top of a ridge. All on board died instantly, a small consolation for the grieving families left behind. Maps have changed since 1949, and Dry Canyon is now called Stone Canyon, where two reservoirs are located, one of which is thought to cover the R4D-6 crash site.

Burned-out wreckage of U.S. Navy Douglas R4D-6, which crashed in the Santa Monica Mountains on July 13, 1949, killing the crew of two and five passengers. *Courtesy D.D. Hatfield Collection.*

Two Vought-designed Corsair fighters, built under license by Goodyear and designated FG-1D, ditched just east of Catalina Island. The first, on August 24, 1949, flown by First Lieutenant Donald H. Clark, USMR, was caused by engine failure. His aircraft ditched successfully just two hundred yards off shore, and he escaped the cockpit before his Corsair sank. The second loss occurred on October 16, and again engine failure forced First Lieutenant Robert R. Lemon, USMCR, to ditch; he also made a successful water landing. His FG-1D stayed afloat for more than a minute, but he went down with it in two hundred fathoms of water. Why would an accomplished marine aviator not be able to exit his aircraft in time to save his life? It has been surmised that following engine failure, First Lieutenant Lemon had his hands full maintaining sufficient airspeed to make a safe landing on the ocean's surface and did not have time to open his canopy and lock it in the open position. Another possibility is that when he ditched his aircraft, he hit the water hard enough to be knocked unconscious or was otherwise incapacitated. Both aircraft suffered loss of power at low altitude, but only one pilot had time to execute all of the protocols required for a safe water landing.

The year 1950 ushered in a new decade, with a substantial increase in air traffic in and around Los Angeles County. As traffic accidents on the county's roadways increased, so they did in the skyways. One notable loss occurred on September 11, 1950, when a war surplus Lockheed Loadstar twin-engine transport owned by famed aviatrix Jacqueline Cochran crashed into 2,714-foot Rocky Peak. The crash killed the crew of two and one passenger. The flight had originated at LAX and was en route to Burbank to pick up two additional passengers, who would then be flown to San Diego for a business meeting. Low stratus clouds covered the Los Angeles Basin, and the Loadstar was flying below the clouds and orbiting over the San Fernando Valley, awaiting landing instructions at Burbank, when it flew into the east face of Rocky Peak. The crash site was a few hundred yards east of the Ventura–Los Angeles county line in extremely rugged and inaccessible terrain. Only the tail assembly and outer wing sections remained intact, and these were later pushed down the mountainside to make the wreck less visible. A yellow X was painted on a large boulder above the main impact to let other flyers know that this was not a missing aircraft. Once again, the low clouds so common in Southern California were a factor.

Knowing when to fly and when to stand down can depend on a host of factors: the weather, the mechanical condition of the aircraft, the qualifications of the pilot or even a premonition of impending doom or

The tail assembly and starboard wing of a Lockheed Loadstar on Rocky Peak. Three died on September 11, 1950, in this weather-related accident. *Courtesy Sewell F. Griggers.*

disaster. The Howard DGA-15-P was a high-wing monoplane powered by a 450-horsepower Wasp Junior radial engine that achieved a cruising speed of 155 miles per hour, making it popular in the postwar years, especially for use as a skydiving platform. DGA-15-P NC- 67765 departed Whiteman Air Park in Pacoima on April 6, 1951, with two married couples on board bound for Las Vegas, Nevada. They disappeared while flying in cloudy but not stormy weather, but the five-seat Howard was not posted missing until April 11. A search effort was mounted along two possible flight routes to Las Vegas; even though the pilot had not filed a flight plan, the Civil Air Patrol expressed confidence that the Howard would be located once weather conditions improved.

The DGA was an acronym for "Darn Good Airplane," and the Howard design was considered a rugged and dependable aircraft. The DGA-15-P was a mostly fabric-covered aircraft, and the missing DGA-15-P had distinctive markings, with fuselage, wings and tail surfaces painted green. The cowling and NC-67765 registration numbers were painted yellow. The wreckage of the Howard was finally located, west of Acton, on April 24, 1951. The plane was discovered by an employee of the Ritter Ranch who was checking

A Howard DGA-15-P, similar to that lost on April 6, 1951, with two married couples on board. *Courtesy William T. Larkins.*

fence lines, and he found four dead bodies in its burned-out wreckage. It was surmised that the pilot was trying to follow the highway from the Newhall Pass to Palmdale and that he became lost in the clouds, crashing into Willow Springs Canyon on Sierra Pelona Ridge.

One of the victims of the crash had lost her first husband in a fatal air crash and, after she remarried, had a child who was eight years old in 1951. Prior to the flight, the victim told a close friend that she had a premonition that something might happen to her—even believing that the colors of the plane she was to fly in were a bad omen. She wrote a will asking that the friend care for her daughter if she did not return. This case raises an interesting question: should we pay heed to our intuition? The burned wreckage of the DGA-15-P is largely undisturbed today, a silent reminder of that tragic day in 1951 when four lives were lost.

When major storms approach Southern California, all too rare an occurrence in recent times, airports and aviators are alerted to the anticipated arrival time, strength and duration of the event. Such was the case in late August 1951, when a subtropical disturbance moving up the coast from Baja California threatened to bring heavy rains and high winds to the Greater Los Angeles area. Commercial flights were rerouted, delayed or canceled. Private planes stayed in their hangars, and those outside had their tie-down cables checked and secured.

SKY'S THE LIMIT!

The U.S. Navy decided to relocate aircraft from Naval Air Station Los Alamitos in Orange County to Moffett Field, some four hundred miles north in the San Francisco Bay area. On August 28, 1951, a flight of six Grumman TBM-3E Avengers departed Los Alamitos NAS at 5:58 p.m., with the leading edge of the storm front already producing rain showers and reducing visibility to one and a half miles. All pilots were briefed to fly to the northern tip of Santa Catalina Island, turn northwest toward Santa Cruz Island and continue on top of the overcast to NAS Moffett Field. Five of the six Avengers had a radar operator on board, but only two units were turned on and one of those was not working properly as the flight headed out to sea.

About fifteen minutes after takeoff the flight entered a heavy rainsquall and was forced to descend to 200 feet. One radar operator reported that the island was dead ahead at two miles, and his pilot started an immediate climb through the overcast, as did three other members of the flight, but there was no response from one pilot, who may not have heard the radio transmission. At 6:13 p.m., two TBM-3Es crashed into Catalina Island, one crashing in a canyon at 1,050 feet MSL and the other near the top of the ridge at 1,300 feet MSL. The two TBM sites are located between the Isthmus and 1,804-foot Silver Peak. Even though both pilots had started a desperate climb to avoid the island, they were not on the assigned heading and could not avoid a collision with the island rising sharply out of the gloom. Four surviving TBM-3Es continued on to NAS Moffett Field, their crews shaken, distressed and mourning the loss of four crewmen who were once a vital part of their V871 squadron. The big storm that threatened Southern California and caused the flight to be made failed to materialize. Fog, rain showers and winds gusting to sixteen miles per hour were all the weakened front produced.

Seldom seen by island visitors, the wreckage sites of the TBM-3Es are scattered in the rough and beautiful country near the west end of Catalina Island. One set of propeller hubs, with blades still attached, is located at the Isthmus, and the other set can be found at Parsons Landing. These propellers are memorials to four navy pilots and air crewmen who lost their lives on August 28, 1951. At the time of this writing, memorial markers are planned for the TBM crewmen.

April 18, 1952, marked the loss of another non-scheduled airliner in Los Angeles County. Robin Air Lines Flight 416W departed New York City on April 16, with stops at Chicago and an eleven-hour delay in Kansas City due to mechanical problems. A precautionary landing at Wichita, Kansas, to check engine oil consumption further slowed the progress of 416W. The flight continued to Amarillo, Texas, and then proceeded to Phoenix, Arizona.

The final leg of the flight departed Phoenix at 1:43 a.m. PST en route to Los Angeles International Airport with twenty-six passengers and a crew of three. Heavy cloud cover blanketed the inland valleys and coastal areas of Southern California, causing the flight crew to file an IFR (instrument flight rules) flight plan for the final thirty-five minutes of the trip. Flight 416W was a World War II surplus C-46F Commando transport and cargo aircraft with the registration number N8404C. While the C-46F lacked radar, air traffic control at LAX had it, and controllers could see the approaching flights about twenty miles from the field. The sophisticated radar systems in place today far exceed the radar technology available in 1952.

As Flight 416W began its descent to land at 3:34 a.m., the controller was watching his screen intently, expecting a blip to appear, but none did. At 3:37 a.m., radio calls were made to 416W, but there was no response. A missing aircraft alert was issued, but early morning fog and low clouds precluded any search flights from being made. At 10:00 a.m. on the morning of April 18, a rancher found the wreckage of N8404C in Puente Hills. The smashed and burned wreckage of the C-46F was strewn over several hundred yards. Investigators found that the landing gear was in the extended or down position, indicating that the crew might have thought they were closer to LAX than they actually were. No one had survived the initial impact, and the CAB concluded that Flight 416W crashed because the pilot had descended below the minimum altitude for which he was cleared and attempted an approach at an altitude too low to clear the terrain.

The author visited the accident site in 1998 and was surprised to find passenger seats, engine ring mounts, parts of the landing gear assemblies, shards of Firestone tires and a substantial amount of aircraft skin, which included trim tabs for the flight control surfaces. Seat belt attachments, a lipstick case, Plexiglas and a host of other small items associated with the C-46F cabin were also present. Chaparral, including poison oak, now covers part of the Puente Hills Habitat Preservation Authority lands on which the site is situated. A housing tract built in the 1960s is a scant four hundred feet away, but the residents seem to be largely unaware of the wreckage and what happened in the early morning hours of April 18, 1952. On a clear day, a visitor can see LAX from the accident site. Just two hundred feet higher, and Flight 416W might have made it all the way to Los Angeles unscathed.

Military transport aircraft experienced losses too. An air force C-47D, 43-48723A departed Norton AFB in San Bernardino County on the evening of June 25, 1952, with a crew of two, as well as five passengers who were to be delivered to the Air National Guard Base at Van Nuys Airport in the

San Fernando Valley. The weather along the flight route included stratus clouds, which were especially thick along the south slopes of the San Gabriel Mountains. The estimated flight time was thirty-five minutes, but when the C-47D failed to arrive as expected and no radio contact could be made, a search effort was launched.

The pilot had filed a VFR (visual flight rules) flight plan at Norton AFB prior to his departure. The fact that the weather conditions were described as being marginal for VFR flight seems to have been overlooked by the pilot. The dense cloud cover hampered aerial search flights until the morning of June 27, when a Civil Air Patrol aircraft spotted the smoldering wreckage of the C-47D just below the east side of Van Tassel Ridge at 3,500 feet MSL. All seven men on board had died upon impact in Angeles National Forest about nine miles north of Monrovia. The air force accident report cited inadequate preflight planning and lack of proper attitude toward flying safety. In 1952, the C-47D wreck was marked with yellow *X*s, denoting that it was a "found" crash site. As the years passed, metal salvagers recovered the aluminum, and a USFS bulldozer buried most of the remaining wreckage in the 1970s.

The Fairchild C-119 Flying Boxcar was the go-to medium-lift tactical transport for the United States Air Force (USAF) in the 1950s. The Boxcar lived up to its name, being able to carry up to sixty-two troops, a 105mm gun or a military truck. The twin-engine, twin-boom design made the C-119 easy to identify. The Boxcar enjoyed a long service life, starting in 1950 and finally retiring in 1975.

The ubiquitous Douglas C-47A Skytrain, whose air force service spanned more than thirty years. Six of these venerable aircraft were lost in mountain crashes within Los Angeles County from 1943 to 1961. *Courtesy William T. Larkins.*

Two air force C-119s were lost in weather-related accidents in Los Angeles County. The first, in 1954, crashed in the Santa Susana Mountains north of Granada Hills on what is now a county park and open-space preserve. The accident occurred on the morning of April 20 as the pilot attempted to make an instrument landing approach at Burbank Airport. The weather included stratus clouds with tops to 2,500 feet and visibility restricted to one mile or less in some areas. The San Fernando Valley was also obscured by smoke, fog and haze, which together would later be described as the bane of the Los Angeles Basin (best known by the portmanteau *smog*).

At 9:28 a.m., the inbound C-119F 51-8153 hit a ridgeline at 2,060 feet, just below 2,771-foot Mission Peak. The flying Boxcar broke up upon impact with the ground, its engines flying off their mounts as the tail booms separated from the center section. The crew of five and two passengers died instantly as their aircraft disintegrated around them. A brush fire touched off by the crash was quickly contained by the Los Angeles County Fire Department. Most of the wreckage was removed by the air force, but hikers making their way up the trail to Mission Peak can still see parts of the C-119F if they know to look on the steep slopes below the trail. The Project Remembrance Team hopes to place a memorial marker at the trailhead reminding the public of the loss of three air force officers and four enlisted ranks on April 20, 1954.

The mid-1950s saw a dramatic increase in air traffic in and around the Greater Los Angeles Basin, and with that increase came a rise in midair collisions. On September 4, 1956, four California Air National Guard F-86A Sabre Jets joined up over the San Gabriel Mountains to practice air combat tactics. During the opening phase of the simulation, two of the F-86As collided just south of 7,124-foot Mount Pacifico, killing one pilot who was unable to escape from his stricken Sabre, although the second pilot managed to eject safely. He was picked up by a rescue helicopter north of Loomis Ranch along the west fork of Alder Creek. The crashes touched off two major forest fires that consumed several thousand acres of the Angeles National Forest. The wrecks of the F-86As were not recovered, and debris from both aircraft, while widely scattered, is still visible in the nooks and crannies of the Alder Creek drainage.

Before any production aircraft can be delivered to the customer, the manufacturer conducts a series of functional test flights that verify the reliability of the controls, airframe, power plants and avionics. Every manufacturer has a cadre of highly skilled "company" test pilots to accomplish this important pre-delivery mission. Tuesday, January 29, 1957, was bright

The Northrop F-89D Scorpion all-weather interceptor, with a crew of two, helped to defend the United States during the Cold War. An F-89J was involved in a midair collision over Pacoima on January 29, 1957. *Courtesy American Aviation Historical Society.*

and clear over Southern California as a Douglas Aircraft Company flight test crew departed Clover Field at 10:15 a.m. in Santa Monica to begin several hours of exhaustive systems checks on a factory-fresh DC-7B slated for delivery to Continental Airlines. Testing of airliners did not require that the crew wear parachutes (though sometimes they would), but on this day, the Douglas men chose not to. Departing Air Force Plant 42 in Palmdale at 10:50 a.m. were two Northrop Aircraft Company employees, pilot Roland E. Owen, and radar technician Curtiss A. Adams, flying a recently modified F-89J Scorpion, 53-24454, all-weather fighter interceptor. Both aircraft were using visual flight rules (VFR), and that meant "see and be seen" for the respective flight crews.

At 11:18 a.m., the outbound DC-7B and the inbound F-89J Scorpion collided nearly head-on over the community of Pacoima in the northeastern part of the San Fernando Valley, with catastrophic results. Without parachutes, the DC-7B crew had no chance to survive, and the F-89J pilot died in the collision; Curtiss A. Adams, his radar test assistant, did manage to eject successfully. Mr. Adams sustained burns and extensive bruising that required hospitalization. The F-89J crew had been tracking another F-89 nearby, testing the newly installed intercept radar, when the collision occurred.

The DC-7B came down on Pacoima Junior High School, injuring seventy-four students and killing three. The nearby Pacoima Congregational Church grounds were also hit by debris from the DC-7B, as were two other nearby schools. One piece of landing gear from the DC-7 crashed into the kitchen of a home, narrowly missing a housewife and her two small children. Parts of the DC-7B and the F-89J were scattered over two miles, with most of the F-89J crashing to earth, with the pilot still in the cockpit, a quarter mile north of La Tuna Canyon Road in the Verdugo Mountains above a county debris basin. Small parts of the F-89J can still be found scattered in the chaparral-covered hillside, a stark reminder that "see and be seen" does not always work.

The "see and be seen" rule can work effectively if speeds are not too great and skies clear, but at night, success can be tenuous at best. On February 1, 1958, at 7:13 p.m., an air force Douglas C-118A 53-3277 Liftmaster collided with a navy Lockheed P2V-5F Bu No 127723 Neptune over the city of Norwalk. The C-118 had departed Long Beach Municipal Airport at 7:08 p.m. en route to McGuire AFB in New Jersey with crew of six and thirty-five

The crash site of the Northrop F-89J 53-24454 in La Tuna Canyon. The F-89J collided with a Douglas DC-7B over Pacoima on January 29, 1957, killing eight people in the air and on the ground. *Courtesy Sewell F. Griggers.*

passengers on board. The P2V-5F also took off at 7:08 p.m., from nearby Los Alamitos Naval Air Station on a night instrument proficiency training flight with a crew of eight.

The collision occurred a mere five minutes after takeoff, causing the C-118A to crash near the intersection of Pioneer and Firestone Boulevards and killing all forty-one men on board. A Norwalk housewife, age twenty-five, was killed as she ran from her house on Jersey Avenue. She was the only victim of the airborne tragedy on the ground. The P2V-5F crashed into a pit where clay was being extracted just off Norwalk Boulevard, across the street from the Los Angeles County Fire Station in Santa Fe Springs. Incredibly, three crewmen of the Neptune survived the initial impact in the clay pit, but one died later at a hospital. Two others—one critically injured, one with minor injuries only—survived the nightmare of falling to earth within the crumpled empennage and tail section of the Neptune patrol bomber. The least injured crewman, a naval reserve aviation machinist mate, was able to climb out of the pit and call for help through a chain link fence to people gathering nearby.

On May 9, 1964, the Norwalk American Legion Post 359 placed a memorial marker in a small shopping center at the northeast corner of Firestone and Pioneer Boulevards near the crash site of the C-118A Liftmaster. The marker lists the names of those who lost their lives while in service to our nation on that fateful evening in February 1958.

The accident investigators found that the pilots failed to see each other, and therefore the cause of the crash was pilot error. At night? Without a warning from ground controllers that other traffic was nearby? Advances in radar technology and the advent of the transponder would greatly reduce (but not entirely eliminate) the risk of midair collisions.

The city of Cerritos experienced an air disaster on August 31, 1986, when Aeromexico Airlines McDonnell Douglas DC-9 Flight 498, en route to LAX, was struck by a Piper PA-28-181 flying to Big Bear Lake, California. The collision resulted in the deaths of all sixty-four passengers and crew aboard Flight 498, the three occupants of the Piper PA-28-181 and fifteen people on the ground. Eight other residents were injured by falling debris. Four homes were completely destroyed, and seven others sustained substantial damage.

The National Transportation Safety Board (NTSB) determined that the accident was caused by the pilot of the Piper PA-28-181 when he flew into restricted airspace. Because the Piper was not equipped with a Mode C Transponder, the TCAS collision avoidance system was not automatically activated. Flight 498 was where it was supposed to be, and the Piper was not. Today, new technological innovations and regulations that require transponders on all aircraft, except those without electrical systems, have helped reduce the risk of such midair collisions.

In March 2006, a memorial sculpture garden was opened to the public at the Cerritos Civic Center honoring the victims of the worst air disaster in the history of Los Angeles County. Designed by noted architect Kathleen Caricof, the memorial was intended to bring a sense of peace and closure to those whose loved ones were tragically lost on that late summer day in 1986.

A North American Aviation F-86L, 51-6006, went down on May 28, 1958, with North American Aviation test pilot Bill Yoakley at the controls. The accident occurred during a routine checkout flight prior to the formal delivery of the F-86L to the air force. The accident was caused by a jet engine flameout over the Catalina Channel. When numerous attempts to restart the J-47 engine failed, Mr. Yoakley was forced to eject at 4,500 feet. The weather and location were perfect for a quick rescue, as dozens of pleasure boats headed toward the descending parachute to assist the pilot, as did an Avalon Air Transport Grumman Goose amphibian, which landed in the ocean nearby and taxied into position to help if needed. It was a navy helicopter in the area that reached Mr. Yoakley first and plucked him from the sea.

The F-86L continued its pilotless glide high over Avalon, finally crashing on the west side of the island. When air force safety investigators were able to visit the crash site a few days later, it was determined that a valve had malfunctioned, shutting off the fuel flow to the engine. In August 1995, the author visited the crash site to photograph the remains of 51-6006 on a mountain ridge southwest of Avalon. With many recognizable parts still visible and scattered across a steep canyon above the Pacific Ocean, the unburned wreckage of the F-86L still shimmered in the summer sun.

Incredibly, from January 1, 1960, until December 31, 1969, there would be more than sixty aircraft accidents on open-space lands and offshore in the Pacific Ocean within the limits of Los Angeles County. There were 101 fatalities, including 15 killed on January 13, 1969, when an SAS Douglas DC-8 airliner made an inadvertent night landing on Santa Monica Bay while approaching LAX. Less than a week later, a United Airlines Boeing 727 crashed into Santa Monica following takeoff from LAX on January 18, 1969, killing all thirty-eight passengers and crew.

Coastal stratus, cumulonimbus and alto-nimbus clouds have been factors in aviation accidents since the earliest days of man-powered flight. There are other clouds—those of smoke, from brush and timber fires—that have

A wing section of air force North American F-86L 51-6006 on Catalina Island; it crashed following engine flameout and successful pilot ejection on May 28, 1958. *G.P. Macha Collection.*

brought aircraft down, along with the fierce winds generated by wildfires that have scarred the mountains and grasslands of Los Angeles County.

The first loss of an airborne firefighting aircraft in Los Angeles County happened on the morning of July 22, 1960. The aircraft, call sign Tanker 66, was a war surplus North American Aviation B-25J Mitchell medium bomber registered as N3446G, for restricted use only. On board were pilot James C. Armstrong and copilot Charles A. Franco. Both men were experienced aviators whose mission was to attack a raging wildfire burning out of control in rugged Mill Canyon northwest of Mount Gleason in the Angeles National Forest. In the early days of aerial firefighting, the use of a lead-in (or guide) aircraft had not yet been adopted. Consequently, the early borate tanker pilots were on their own in terms of how best to attack the fire. When dense smoke and the erratic fire-generated winds were added to the mix, the risk factors for tanker pilots were exponentially increased. Firefighters nearby saw Tanker 66 fly up Mill Canyon and disappear into the thick smoke. When the B-25J failed to emerge moments later, the fire boss informed the Los Angeles County Sheriff's Department that Tanker 66 had crashed.

The wreckage of the B-25J was reached the following day at 4,500 feet MSL in Mill Canyon, about 500 feet below the top of a ridgeline that Tanker 66 would have had to clear. The bodies of both victims were recovered and the wreckage abandoned in its hard-to-see resting place. In

North American Aviation B-25J N3446G call sign Tanker 66 was photographed at Chino Airport a few months before it crashed on July 22, 1960. *Photo by Milo Peltzer.*

The crash site of Tanker 66 in Mill Canyon of the Angeles National Forest, with Pat J. Macha holding a rudder section from the B-25J N3446G. *Photo by Rich Allison.*

spite of the post-impact fire, much of Tanker 66 remained intact, including the wings, empennage and distinctive twin tails, a hallmark of the B-25 Mitchell bomber. By the 1990s, warbird restorers were visiting the crash site of Tanker 66 to recover useful parts, but enough material is still there to make Tanker 66 visible on Google Earth.

The second loss of an aerial first responder happened at 11:50 a.m. on September 27, 1960, when a war surplus single-engine Grumman TBM-3E Avenger, N9598C, piloted by William F. Druehl, crashed while fighting a brush fire above Altadena. Mr. Druehl had flown five successful borate drops on the Brown Mountain fire when he radioed that he could not open the dump doors for the sixth drop of the day. Haze and smoke obscured the drop zone, and when the Tanker failed to return to its base, a search was launched.

The wrecked Grumman was found on the afternoon of the twenty-seventh by a helicopter flying a fire-related support mission. When Sergeant C. Lyndall Griggers of the LCSD aviation unit arrived at the TBM crash site, the body of the pilot was found slumped over in the cockpit. The wreck of the TBM-3E N9598C is situated in a narrow recess of El Prieto Canyon on the south flank of Brown Mountain and is visible today on Google Earth.

When the author visited the crash site in the late 1960s, a couch was found in the cockpit behind the pilot. Confused at first, the author later found out that Mr. Druehl had rested on it between fire attack missions. Today, the wreck of

The Grumman TBM-3E N9598C converted for use as an aerial tanker. This aircraft was lost on a firefighting mission on September 27, 1960. *Courtesy Milo Peltzer Collection.*

The empennage section with tail wheel assembly of TBM-3E N9598C in rugged El Prieto Canyon on Brown Mountain in the Angeles National Forest. *Photo by Pat J. Macha.*

the TBM-3E is slowly being buried by silt from runoff, as well as by rock falls. The losses of the aerial first responders are not unlike those lost in war, and they should be honored as any veteran of battle who faces death and injury. In these battles, the fire attack pilots and their crews face the indiscriminate enemies of topography, wind and fire. Since 1960, fifteen men have died in firefighting-related air crashes in Los Angeles County.

The Lockheed F-104 Starfighter was manufactured by Lockheed Aircraft in Burbank, but most of the final assembly and subsequent flight tests were conducted at Air Force Plant 42 in Palmdale. The Starfighter was also known as "the zipper" and "the missile with a man in it." The F-104 could achieve speeds of 1,150 miles per hour and altitudes above fifty thousand feet. Impressive and ahead of its time, the Starfighter served the USAF and many of our allies well. A few were loaned to the U.S. Navy to test the effectiveness of the AIM-9 Sidewinder heat-seeking air-to-air missile. All Sidewinder tests were conducted at the China Lake Naval Ordinance Test Station near Ridgecrest, California.

On September 22, 1960, USMC captain Howard O. Casada Jr. was flying F-104A 56-0740 with two Sidewinder missiles carrying inert warheads when he became unconscious due to the failure of the oxygen system. His aircraft, out of control and traveling at a high rate of speed, impacted the south face of 5,558-foot Josephine Peak in the San Gabriel Mountains. The explosion and shockwave from the crash of the F-104A was felt and heard more than twenty-five miles away. The Starfighter wreck site was easily located by rescue personnel due to the brush fire that had been ignited. After the fire had been contained, military investigators visited the site over many days looking for the pilot's remains, as well as any classified components that might have survived, but almost nothing was found. One deputy sheriff described the scene as "confetti strewn on [the] mountainside in an almost perfect circle."

Today, the crash site is overgrown by chaparral in a rock garden that most hikers avoid. One accomplished mountaineer and canyoneer, Matt Maxon, not only reached the F-104A site but also went to the Los Angeles Board of Supervisors to ask that the canyon below the Starfighter wreckage be named in memory of Marine Corps captain Howard O. Casada. Thanks to the support of Supervisor Michael D. Antonovich, the board of supervisors voted unanimously to support the measure. Ask almost any mountain biker or hiker en route to Josephine Peak what canyon they are riding or hiking in, and the answer will be, "Casada!"

Low coastal clouds and darkness were factors in the September 20, 1961 loss of USAF Douglas C-47A 43-16002 on 3,747-foot Oat Mountain, the highest point in the Santa Susana Mountains. Based at Oxnard AFB in Ventura County, 43-16002 departed at 6:42 p.m. on a routine training flight to Palmdale, where the crew would practice touch-and-go landings and takeoffs until 9:02 p.m. En route back to Oxnard AFB, the crew encountered dense cloud cover that obscured the Santa Clarita and San Fernando Valleys. Nonetheless, they continued westward under visual flight rules (VFR). At 9:26 p.m., the C-47A collided with terrain at 3,200-foot MSL.

The C-47A had crashed on a dirt road and careened onto a gentle slope inhabited by grazing cattle and oak trees. Three of the crew members, including the pilot and copilot, were killed in the crash, but two officers and one sergeant survived with moderate to minor injuries. The three survivors managed to walk down a road toward the San Fernando Valley, where they stumbled into an army radar site for a Nike antiaircraft missile installation at 6:30 a.m. The wreckage was almost entirely removed in the weeks following the accident, reducing C-47A to a micro site.

United Air Lines (UAL) is best known for serving cities nationwide, but it was also a major intercity passenger carrier in the state of California during the 1960s. Using the twin-engine Convair Model 340 medium-range

The demolished wreck of USAF Douglas C-47A 43-16002 on Oat Mountain, where three crewmen died and three survived on September 20, 1961. *Courtesy Sewell F. Griggers.*

airliner, United had flights connecting a dozen cities within California. These flights were extensively used by businessmen and businesswomen to get to destinations quickly and efficiently. UAL Convair 340 N73102, Flight 593, departed Reno, Nevada, on the morning of December 30, 1964, with a stop at Fresno, California, before continuing to Los Angeles International Airport. With forty-three passengers and a crew of four on board, the Convair 340 climbed out of Fresno on what should have been an hour-and-fifteen-minute flight to LAX. Flight 593 flew south over the San Joaquin Valley without incident and then gained additional altitude to cross the Tehachapi Mountains, flying over the 4,144-foot Tejon Pass, straddled by peaks up to 8,000 feet. Shortly after clearing the top of the pass, Captain William M. "Bill" Wade began a gradual descent as he headed toward LAX following Highway 99 (Interstate 5). Clouds covered the flight route ahead and light rain was falling, the harbinger of a major winter storm that was expected the next day.

SKY'S THE LIMIT!

Suddenly, both of the Pratt & Whitney R-2800 engines on the Convair 340 quit. Captain Wade and his first officer, Jerry J. Campbell, followed the UAL checklist to attempt engine restart while making sure the remaining fuel was being pumped to the engines. A fuel pump malfunction had caused fuel starvation to stop both R-2800s. Descending at 180 miles per hour in IFR conditions, the Convair broke through the clouds at the north end of the Santa Clarita Valley. Captain Wade realized that his only chance was to attempt an emergency landing at a closed airstrip then being used as farmland. With his landing gear retracted and flaps partially lowered, Captain Wade made a successful dead stick landing. All of the crew and forty-one passengers walked away, shaken but otherwise unhurt. Only two passengers sustained minor injuries in this landing on the only safe open space for miles around.

Among the grateful survivors of Flight 593 were Mr. and Mrs. Martin Matich, who later told their son, Stephen, that they expected to die in the crash. They prayed together that their deaths would be as quick and painless as possible. With seat belts tightened and holding hands, they rode out the rough and bumpy landing without injury. The Matich family and most of the other survivors completed their trip by bus into Los Angeles. Martin Matich at the time of the accident was president of the Matich Corporation, well known for constructing airport runways, tarmacs, highways and freeways.

Captain Wade landed on what had been the Newhall Airport, used by airlines from the 1930s through the late 1940s as an emergency landing field if Burbank or Grand Central Airports were fogged in. The field closed in 1952, but thankfully, it remained open space. The initial post-accident investigation cited pilot error related to a fuel management issue, but that was changed. There was an error in the United Air Lines training manual regarding fuel cross-feed procedures, and it was quickly modified following this incident.

Captain Wade and his first officer, Jerry Campbell, continued to fly for United Airlines for many years after their forced landing. Bill Wade retired as a Boeing 747 captain. The fate of the wrecked Convair 340 N73102 is a remarkable one. Once the mechanics and inspectors evaluated the airframe, it was decided to jack the aircraft up, repair damage to the fuselage skin, replace the engines and propellers and, with a reduced fuel load, fly the plane to LAX for a major refit. Bulldozers graded a new runway that was compacted by rollers, and in January 1965, an uneventful takeoff was made. Several months later, N73102 was returned to service with United Airlines.

The United Air Lines Convair 340 was used extensively as a regional carrier serving LAX, Fresno, Sacramento, San Francisco and other smaller cities within California during the 1960s. *Photo by UAL official via American Aviation Historical Society.*

Pilot skill and good luck paid off in a miracle landing with engines out on a UAL Convair 340 near Newhall, California, on December 30, 1964. *Photo by UAL official via D.D. Hatfield Collection.*

A storm front following United Flight 593 had arrived over Southern California as a Beechcraft T-34A Mentor N5506V departed Edwards Air Force Base on December 31, 1964, en route to San Diego with two men on board. The T-34A was owned by the base flying club. The pilot filed a VFR flight plan, even though IFR conditions were anticipated along the flight route. Crossing the San Gabriel Mountains could be especially dangerous in the conditions forecast on the day of the flight. When the T-34A failed to arrive at the destination indicated, a search effort was launched; however, snow was falling in the mountains, and many search flights were curtailed. Nonetheless, the Civil Air Patrol and sheriff aviation units from three counties participated in search efforts for several weeks without success. As spring approached, it was hoped that the crash site of the T-34A would be found, but this was not the case. Following the spring snowmelt, there was still no success until a hiker going overland from Grassy Hollow Camp Ground on Highway 2 to Jackson Lake stumbled upon the smashed wreckage of N5506V on July 31, 1965.

NTSB investigators, members of the Los Angeles County Sheriff's Department and the Los Angeles County Coroner were amazed to find that the T-34A was only a few hundred yards from Highway 2. Why had it not been seen? It was buried in snow for several months and then, in spring and summer, camouflaged by the trees and undergrowth in a small hollow.

The NTSB accident report for N5506V cited IFR conditions and uncontrolled descent. It was surmised that the pilot was trying to fly across the San Gabriel Mountain Range between 10,064-foot Mount San Antonio and 9,407-foot Mount Baden-Powell at Vincent Gap. Had he cleared Lightning Ridge, he might have made it.

The case was solved, families of the deceased had closure and the black-and-yellow T-34A was marked with Xs and forgotten about until many years later, when a lightning strike caused a fire near the site. When the firefighters arrived, they found aircraft wreckage, and some thought that it must be a missing aircraft. Once again, representatives of various government agencies were required to certify that this was the T-34A and not an unknown or missing aircraft. The fire had burned the paint off the T-34A, but much of it remains now, and when the sunlight is just right, the reflection from aluminum parts can still be seen from Highway 2, but only if you know where to look.

Weather conditions for airmen flying into or out of the Los Angeles Basin on March 27, 1966, were described as "adverse." One pilot departed Bakersfield at about 6:00 a.m. en route to Hawthorne Airport, and when he

Bob and Herb Lank with a tail section of the Cessna 172D N2958U, which crashed during a rainstorm on March 27, 1966, killing the pilot. *Photo by G.P. Macha.*

failed to arrive as planned, a search was launched. Poor weather hindered search efforts, but on March 30, the burned-out wreckage of the missing Cessna 172D N2958U was found in a rugged area of the San Gabriel Mountains near Big Tujunga Canyon road and the southwest flank of 4,705-foot Magic Mountain. Heavy rain along with the pilot not being instrumented rated were cited by the NTSB as factors in the accident. The wreck was marked with black *X*s, and on April 12, 1968, the author and two young brothers-in-law hiked through chaparral and white thorn to visit what remained of Cessna 172. It is still visible today from the roadway, as well as on Google Earth.

Eight miles west of the once missing T-34A crash is Pallet Mountain. Hikers climbing nearby Mount Williamson sometimes hike over to Pallet Mountain for the fine views of the Antelope Valley and the Great Mojave Desert. Other hikers make the trek to visit the crash site of a USAF C-119G that lies along the 7,830-foot ridgeline east of the mountain's summit.

On the night of September 30, 1966, four air force reservists assigned to the 730th Troop Carrier Squadron at March AFB in Riverside County were ordered to fly a VFR night proficiency training mission to Palmdale Airport in Los Angeles County. The C-119G 53-3195 departed March AFB at 6:33 p.m. with Major Alvin O. Estes as pilot and Captain Norman

The Fairchild C-119G Flying Boxcar served with the air force as a medium-lift transport from 1949 until 1975. Serial number 53-3195 crashed on Pallet Mountain, killing the four-man crew on September 30, 1966. *Courtesy William T. Larkins.*

M. Grossman and Captain Raymond L. Miller, who were both pilots, taking turns flying as copilots. Staff Sergeant Roger C. Du Charme was crew chief. All radio messages received both by RAPCON military radar controllers and Federal Aviation Administration (FAA) controllers were normal, and no problems were indicated by the crew of the Flying Boxcar. At about 9:15 p.m., radar contact with C-119G 53-3195 was lost, as the aircraft had collided with a ridgeline east of Pallet Mountain at 7,832 feet MSL. All four crewmen were killed as the Flying Boxcar's flight deck plunged several feet down into a steep draw on the southeast side of the ridge.

Rescue efforts were launched by the air force, and the USFS dispatched a Bell 47 G-3B1 N1166W helicopter with a pilot and two firefighters on board to knock down hot spots from a five-acre fire caused by the C-119G crash. As the Bell helicopter approached the crash site, it lost power, causing the helicopter to crash at Islip Saddle and Highway 2. Even though the Bell 47 G-3B1 tumbled down 150 feet into Islip Canyon, all three men escaped without major injuries. The twisted wreckage of the helicopter remained undisturbed until about 2008, when most of it was salvaged.

The air force accident report for C-119G 53-3195 cited darkness and clouds as factors. The tragic loss of four men on a "routine" training mission left grieving families and friends. The author climbed to the crash site with Los Angeles Parks ranger Jack Farley Jr. and the author's son in the fall of 1986. We took some time to reflect on the loss of the crew, the impact of

The port wing of air force C-119G 53-3195, with faded national insignia, on Pallet Mountain. *Photo by G.P. Macha.*

A C-119G starboard tail boom, with vertical stabilizer and rudder attached. *Photo by G.P. Macha.*

their passing on their respective families and what could have been if they had been just 150 feet higher.

The C-119G is the largest still visible crash site in Los Angeles County. It can be seen from the desert below and from passing aircraft except when winter snows blanket the wreck. The C-119G is also visible on Google Earth, sharing the same mountain as the C-46A loss of February 20, 1943.

While fixed-wing air tankers carry the greatest volume of Phos-Chek (the replacement for Borate), used in attacking fires, helicopters are utilized more frequently for their ability to attack one hot spot and to carry firefighters to and from locations inaccessible to vehicles. Yet rotary-wing aircraft have become the first responders to most wildfires. They have been an essential component to aerial firefighting since the mid-1960s, but not without losses.

Helicopter pilot Donald Hardenberg was working as a contract pilot for the USFS when he was killed on August 26, 1968, while fighting a fire near Highway 39, 1.5 miles north of the San Gabriel Canyon Reservoir. He was flying a French-built Alouette III turbine-powered jet helicopter. Mr. Hardenberg was attacking a fire that had killed eight firefighters on the ground just two days earlier. On August 30, a Bell 47G-2 crashed while fighting a stubborn blaze north of the Cogswell Reservoir, nine miles west of the Alouette III crash site, seriously injuring the pilot.

Aircraft accidents in Los Angeles County open-space areas from 1970 to 1979 included 106 lives lost and 44 aircraft destroyed or heavily damaged. The disappearance of Beechcraft Bonanza N618V on February 9, 1970, with a man on board led to an immediate aerial search due to the pilot's distress call. N618V crashed en route from Daggett on the Mojave Desert to Hawthorne Municipal Airport in the Greater Los Angeles Basin. The pilot radioed that he was experiencing engine problems while flying over the San Gabriel Mountains. On February 11, the Civil Air Patrol spotted the virtually intact Bonanza in a saddle near Iron Mountain, west of 10,064-foot Mount San Antonio. A sheriff's helicopter landed next to the Bonanza and found the pilot deceased inside. The NTSB investigators found that a combination of fuel mismanagement and spatial disorientation factored in the accident. N618V remained undisturbed for some time but was finally removed by a heavy-lift helicopter.

The loss on June 6, 1971, of Hughes Air West DC-9-31 jetliner Flight 706 following a midair collision also resulted in the losses of all forty-nine passengers and crew. Flight 706 had been airborne less than twenty minutes after departing LAX en route to Salt Lake City, Utah, when it was struck by a marine jet. The pilot of the marine McDonnell Douglas F-4B Phantom II

The Beechcraft Bonanza N618V on Iron Mountain in the Angeles National Forest. *Photo by NTSB official.*

was killed as his aircraft collided with the forward fuselage of the DC-9-31, with catastrophic results. The marine radar intercept officer (RIO) in the backseat of the F-4B managed to eject safely, sustaining only minor injuries. Both aircraft plunged into the San Gabriel Mountains, with the F-4B striking Mount Bliss and the DC-9-31 crashing above nearby Fish Canyon, touching off a brush and timber fire. The crash sites of both aircraft could be seen burning from the San Gabriel Valley towns of Monrovia and Duarte.

The work of first responders was hampered by steep terrain, dense chaparral and fire burning at the respective crash sites. Only the tail assembly of the DC-9-31 remained partially intact and unburned. An effort to remove it by a heavy-lift helicopter failed, and the tail remains a silent sentinel overlooking the main impact of Flight 706. Few hikers have attempted to reach the crash site of Flight 706, and those who have describe almost impenetrable chaparral, with poison oak a prolific hazard of the hike.

The NTSB accident report stated that a combination of factors was responsible for this midair collision. The NTSB cited the marine F-4B Bu No 151458 that was returning from a combat training mission in Nevada, en route to its home base at MCAS El Toro in Orange County, California. The NTSB report noted that the oxygen system on the F-4B had failed, requiring the crew to fly at lower-than-normal altitudes. The second factor was that the F-4B's transponder was inoperable, making the F-4B almost invisible on ATC radar screens. The third factor was that the marine pilot did not contact air traffic control as he entered the Los Angeles Basin to request a radar advisory. Because of the speeds both jets were traveling, neither pilot would have been able to see and avoid the other. The collision occurred at 15,150 feet, with some passengers and crew being thrown out of the DC-9-31N9345. As a result of this tragic accident, the NTSB recommended a number of actions, including better cooperation between military RAPCON controllers and FAA ATC controllers and improved navigational charts to better define high-traffic routes in civilian airspace. The ultimate outgrowth in attempting to prevent midair collisions was the development of both TCAS (traffic alert collision avoidance systems) and ACAS (airborne collision avoidance systems). These technologies are being used extensively today on a worldwide basis, and transponders are mandated for all aircraft in the United States.

Accidents can occur in all types of aircraft, regardless of size, type or function, and that includes sailplanes, too. For many decades, soaring has been a popular aviation pastime in Los Angeles County. The majority of glider flights in Los Angeles County originate from airfields located in the Antelope Valley, where the San Gabriel Mountains are only a few minutes' flying time away. On October 9, 1971, a Schemp Cirrus sailplane crashed on 9,407-foot Mount Baden Powell at 9,000 feet MSL. Witnesses saw the sailplane cross a ridge and then turn to cross it again when the Cirrus struck trees and crashed, killing the pilot. Another wrecked sailplane is located on a ridge south of Baden Powell, but the history of this loss is unknown at the time of writing. The Cirrus N6664 is visible on Google Earth.

Another sailplane wreck visible on Google Earth is that of a Schweizer 2-32 N7622, which crash-landed in the bottom of Vincent Gulch on February 6, 1974. The cause of the accident is attributed to severe downdrafts, but good piloting and luck saved the pilot and his passenger. Both men emerged from their destroyed glider with minor injuries. Those hiking into the lower reaches of the gulch will pass by this interesting and unmarked site, and in doing so, they will also pass the rotor blades of a Sikorsky H-19 helicopter from a non-fatal 1950s crash landing. Another half dozen sailplane wrecks litter the San Gabriel Mountains, most of which were not survivable.

On August 26, 1976, Lady Luck smiled on another pilot flying a Cessna 150K over Vincent Gulch when he hit trees and crashed near Vincent Gap, just below Highway 2. On August 27, a motorist driving on the Angeles Crest Highway saw an aircraft wing hanging in a tree and notified authorities.

Pat J. Macha sits in a wrecked Schweizer 2-32 sailplane that crashed in Vincent Gulch on February 6, 1974. *Photo by Tom Gossett.*

Incredibly, the pilot, who had spent a night in the mountains, was rescued, though with serious injuries.

From 1980 to 1989, there were forty aircraft accidents and fifty-seven fatalities on Los Angeles County open-space lands. The greatest loss of life happened at the Santa Catalina Island Airport on January 30, 1984. At about 1:30 p.m. a Model 24 Lear Jet N44GA attempted a landing but overran runway 22, descending off a ninety-foot bluff and impacting on the terrain below. The flight crew of two and four passengers perished in the accident. According to the NTSB report, N44GA was destroyed by severe impact forces and a post-impact fire. The NTSB report concluded that the Lear Jet could have landed safely but that there was no margin for error. The reason for the accident is officially "undetermined." Micro parts of three other civilian aircraft can still be seen off the end of runway 22, reminders of the skill and good judgment required to effect a safe landing anywhere, not just at Catalina Island Airport.

The years between 1990 and 2000 witnessed a reduction in aviation accidents and fatalities within the county, with twenty-one accidents and twenty-six fatalities. Nine crashes occurred on Santa Catalina Island and three in the Santa Monica Mountains.

One of the Catalina accidents was a runway overrun incident similar to that of the Lear Jet. The accident date was August 4, 1996, and involved a Cessna 421C N6209V with six passengers and one pilot. Thankfully, this accident did not become a tragedy, as three passengers survived with minor injuries and three others and the pilot sustained serious but survivable injuries. The NTSB investigation concluded that the Cessna's landing speed may have been too fast and that the aircraft may have touched down too long on the runway.

The Lockheed C-130 Hercules series of turbo-prop medium-lift transport aircraft has been in continuous production since 1954. Lockheed Martin continues to produce the rugged and dependable Hercules at the company's Marietta, Georgia facility. The C-130 has served in more than sixty-three nations, and more than 2,500 have been manufactured. Used primarily in the United States by the air force, it also serves with marines and the coast guard. Civilian cargo versions are also in service, and the C-130 is

Opposite, bottom: A wing from a Cessna 150K hangs in a tree below Highway 2. Incredibly, the pilot survived the crash, though with serious injuries, on August 26, 1976. *Photo by G.P. Macha.*

currently used as an aerial firefighter, flown by the air national guard; the forest service also operated early production C-130A aircraft, leased from private operators.

C-130A N135FF was owned and operated by Hemet Valley Flying Service, a company with a long history in aerial firefighting. N135FF departed Hemet-Ryan Airport in Riverside County, California, on August 13, 1994, with a crew of three. The C-130A was en route to fight a fire burning in the Tehachapi Mountains of Kern County. The C-130A was observed crossing the San Gabriel Mountains, where it was seen exploding and crashing on Pleasant View Ridge south of the community of Pearblossom, touching off a brush fire. When first responders arrived, they saw that the starboard wing was about 1,000 feet from the main impact area of the fuselage and port (or left) wing. The crash occurred at about 1:30 p.m., and the post-impact fire could be easily seen over a wide area of Antelope Valley. The crash site location, at about 6,600 feet MSL near the top of Pechner Canyon, could only be easily reached by helicopter.

The loss of Tanker 82 claimed the lives of pilot Robert L. Buc, copilot Joe Johnson and flight engineer Shawn Zaremba, all of whom were experienced and respected members of the aerial firefighting community. As families grieved, the NTSB attempted to determine the exact cause of the C-130A loss and that of its crew.

A Lockheed C-130A N135FF photo taken at Porterville Airport a few days before its tragic loss on August 13, 1994. *Photo by Milo Peltzer.*

Structural failure was suspected, as were the consequences of a possible engine fire, but it was not until the June 17, 2002 loss of C-130A N130HP while fighting a wildfire near Walker, California, that NTSB investigator George Petterson suspected that there could a relationship between the Tanker 82 loss and that of N130HP. Three aircrews were killed when the starboard wing of their C-130A Tanker 130 failed in flight, in full view of firefighters on the ground. George Petterson was assigned to the Hawkins & Powers Aviation C-130A loss and found evidence that failure to follow mandated Federal Aviation Administration directives and maintenance procedures were responsible for the catastrophic failure of the C-130A wing structure. Mr. Petterson then requested a revisit to the Tanker 82 crash site, where he found evidence of the same cracks in its wing structure, too. Once his reports were filed and reviewed, the FAA ordered all C-130A aircraft grounded.

Two cases were resolved, and the need to increase inspections on aircraft with high wing loading—where fatigue cracks and corrosion issues would be detected before an accident—helped make flying fire attack aircraft significantly safer. Mr. Petterson was presented with a lifetime achievement award at the Aviation Week & Space Technology 2004 Laureates Award dinner in Washington, D.C., for his accomplishments in aviation safety and accident prevention. In 2014, Mr. Petterson was honored by the Aerial Firefighters Association with the first-ever Walt Darren Award for his groundbreaking work on the Tanker 82 and Tanker 130 accidents. In 2009, the author was flown over the C-130A crash site by master pilot Mr. George Petterson. The C-130A is still visible from the air and also on Google Earth.

The work of aerial first responders is often dangerous and sometimes deadly, as noted by the loss of a Civil Air Patrol Cessna 182R N9706E search aircraft and its three-man crew. When the CAP flight departed Cable Airport in San Bernardino County at 10:30 a.m. on January 14, 1995, it was tasked with searching an area of the San Gabriel Mountains between the community of Wrightwood and 10,064-foot Mount San Antonio. The CAP men were looking for a Cessna 182B N2569G that was last seen flying in the Wrightwood area on December 31, 1994, with one man on board.

All three men on the CAP 182R were experienced pilots, trained in mountain flying and search and rescue (SAR) techniques. At 11:36 a.m., another CAP pilot reported receiving emergency locator transmitter (ELT) signals east of his search location. At about this same time, Cessna 182R disappeared from ATC radar. In spite of clouds and strong downdrafts

C-130A N135FF wreckage on Pleasant View Ridge following wing separation on August 13, 1994. *Courtesy George Peterson.*

A propeller blade and hub from C-130A N135FF on Pleasant View Ridge. *Courtesy George Peterson.*

reported in the area of the ELT signals, a Los Angeles County Sheriff's Department Sikorsky S-58T helicopter was able to find the wrecked Cessna and lower a rescue team to locate survivors. Unfortunately, CAP pilot Captain Robert A. Leman and observers Captain James C. Spadafore and Lieutenant Brian Perkins were killed in the crash. The recovery of the deceased Civil Air Patrol crew had to wait until improved weather conditions on January 15 allowed the grim mission to be completed.

The recovery of the Cessna 182R wreckage, located at 7,700 feet MSL southwest of 9,648-foot Pine Mountain, was effected on September 6, 1995, via helicopter. A gathering was held in February 1995 in Upland to honor the memory of the lost CAP crew and the many first responders who risked their lives to locate the crashed Cessna and recover the bodies of the crewmen.

The search for the missing Cessna 182B continued on an off-and-on basis until September 25, 1995, when a hiker stumbled upon the crash site on the southeast slope of rugged Cucamonga Peak in San Bernardino County. Finding the remains of pilot Terry Corkhill, the hiker contacted the San Bernardino County Sheriff's Department. The ELT in the C-182B had failed to transmit signals due to a post-impact fire. The emergency locator transmitter has saved many lives and shortened many searches since the inception of the device in the 1970s. However, if the ELT antenna is separated or damaged in the crash, or if the ELT is damaged by fire or not properly maintained, the transmitter will not function as expected. The C-182B is another crash site visible on Google Earth.

Improved training techniques, coupled with advances in aviation-related technologies, continue to improve flying safety and help reduce the number of accidents. Accidents on Los Angeles County open-space lands and offshore waters totaled twenty-two, with thirty-two fatalities from January 1, 2000, through mid-2014.

Nine of the twenty-first-century accidents in the county occurred on Santa Catalina Island or the Pacific Ocean nearby. The first incident involved a Piper PA-32, called the Cherokee Six because it could accommodate a pilot and five passengers. On November 3, 2001, PA-32-260 N3516W departed the Catalina Island Airport with a pilot and two passengers en route to McClellan-Palomar Airport near Carlsbad in San Diego County. Shortly after takeoff, the 260-horsepower, six-cylinder Lycoming engine lost power for reasons that were never determined. Nonetheless, the pilot made a textbook ditching two miles east of the Isthmus, near Rippers Cove. Fortunately, there were boaters nearby, and the first to reach the scene was a sailboat owner who was enjoying a ride in his motorized dinghy. Seeing the Piper land on the water, he sped to the rescue, reaching the three survivors within moments and pulling all three individuals aboard his dinghy. Also coming to assist was a forty-five-foot powerboat that took the survivors to the Catalina Isthmus for a medical checkup by Baywatch paramedics before returning to the mainland. Most of the baggage from the Cherokee Six was recovered by divers within a week and returned to the owners. The Piper is reported to be resting on the sea floor, visible from the ocean surface in the clear waters off Catalina Island.

The accidents that followed on the island resulted in the deaths of seventeen persons and serious injuries for eight others. The factors in these accidents included (two) runway overruns; (two) takeoff accidents; (two) weather issues, not near the airport; (one) pilot with a medical issue; and (one) engine malfunction involving a helicopter.

Remarkable stories of survival always receive the public's attention, as well they should. A forty-five-minute scenic glider ride from Crystalaire Airport near the high desert community of Llano took an unusual turn on December 3, 2005. The German-built two-seat Burkhart Grob sailplane was towed aloft at 2:30 p.m. with a female glider pilot and male passenger to begin a soaring adventure over the snow-covered San Gabriel Mountains. After thirty minutes of smooth air and uneventful flying, strong downdrafts were encountered. The pilot attempted to find the updrafts needed to gain sufficient altitude to safely cross a mountain ridge blocking her route back to Crystalaire Airport. When the sailplane continued to lose altitude, another option had to be quickly selected. Remaining calm, she advised her passenger that they needed to make an emergency landing, and within moments, she piloted the Burkhart Grob up a mountainside to a safe landing. Neither the pilot nor her passenger sustained any injuries, but they were now in a remote location, and the declining temperature at high altitude would soon be their greatest concern.

When the sailplane failed to return to Crystalaire Airport by 4:00 p.m. the Los Angeles County Sheriff's Department was notified, as was the Civil Air Patrol. Gusty winds blew that night over the San Gabriel Mountains, and temperatures dropped into the low twenty-degree range. Shortly after dawn on December 4, two sheriff's helicopters began searching the canyons and peaks south of Llano. At 7:20 a.m., the owner of the glider school (and grandfather of the missing glider pilot), along with one observer, spotted the crashed sailplane. A sheriff's helicopter arrived shortly thereafter, lifting both survivors to safety and leading to a tearful reunion with family and friends.

The intact but structurally damaged Burkhart Grob G103 Twin II sailplane, N4601M, was recovered by helicopter from the Pinyon Ridge area of the Angeles National Forest. Even in the twenty-first century, takeoffs are still optional, but landings are always mandatory.

CHAPTER 4

THE MISSING

HOW THEY HAUNT US

Aircraft flying over Los Angeles County have vanished without an apparent trace. Sometimes extensive ground, sea and air searches have come to naught despite hundreds of flight hours by air force, navy, coast guard, civil air patrol and the Los Angeles County Sheriffs' Aviation Unit.

In 1935, the Northrop Aircraft Corporation entered a competition for a new U.S. Army Air Corps fighter aircraft with a design designation of Northrop 3A. The all-metal, single-seat, low-wing design featured retractable landing gear, an enclosed cockpit and a seven-hundred-horsepower Pratt & Whitney Twin Wasp Jr. power plant. Armament included two 0.30-inch or two 0.50-inch machine guns. The 3A had a top speed at sea level of 279 miles per hour, but early test flights indicated stability problems and a propensity to spin. Nonetheless, test flights were ordered to continue so that modifications could be made to the design. The dimensions of the 3A included a scant thirty-two-foot wingspan and a twenty-three-foot length.

The next series of test flights was to be flown by army reserve First Lieutenant Arthur H. Skaer Jr. Lieutenant Skaer was also the Northrop Company test pilot. He was married, lived in the Los Angeles area and was considered a good pilot by his peers. A test flight from Mines Field (LAX) was scheduled for Tuesday afternoon, July 30, 1935. Lieutenant Skaer wore a military-style flying outfit that included khaki pants, street shoes, leather jacket and leather helmet with goggles attached. When Lieutenant Skaer climbed into the cockpit of the 3A, he appeared confident and businesslike. The Northrop Factory photographer was on hand as Lieutenant Skaer

First Lieutenant Arthur H. Skaer Jr. makes a dramatic flyby at Mines Field (LAX) on July 30, 1935, prior to commencing a flight test program from which he never returned. *Courtesy Roy L. Wolford Collection.*

taxied to the end of the grass and dirt runway and performed an engine runup. Checking for other traffic, he turned into the wind and let his engine roar. The diminutive pursuit plane rose quickly from Mines Field and then banked to the left; turning again, he flew east and then turned once more, coming around for a high-speed flyby. Photos taken at the time depict a pilot wanting to be seen, his canopy open, flying fifty feet off the ground straight toward the sand dunes west of Mines Field and the Pacific Ocean beyond. Lieutenant Skaer's mission was to familiarize himself with the 3A prior to a series of demonstration flights that he was scheduled to perform for army representatives at Wright Field in Dayton, Ohio.

Test flights in the modern era require a chase aircraft to observe prototype aircraft in all aspects of its flight regimen, but in the 1930s, that was not the case. When the 3A failed to return to Mines Field by 3:00 p.m., four army observation planes from Long Beach Municipal Airport took off in an effort to locate the errant pursuit plane. The army planes, each with a crew of two, searched the area around the Palos Verdes Hills and then continued north along the coastline of Santa Monica Bay. As the afternoon wore on, coastal stratus clouds began their late afternoon and evening encroachment, but no sign of the 3A or its pilot turned up. In the days that followed Lieutenant Skaer's disappearance, reports streamed in, including sightings of an oil slick in the kelp off Palos Verdes Peninsula and fishermen who saw the 3A flying into the fog near Malibu. The discovery of an aviator's leather flying helmet on the shoreline near Point Vicente on Palos Verdes was proved later not to be that worn by Lieutenant Skaer.

A news flash that aircraft wreckage had been found on San Clemente Island on August 2 gave hope that the mystery of the Northrop 3A would be solved. The wreckage in a rugged canyon turned out to be that of a biplane that crashed in November 1934 while taking goat hunters to San Clemente Island. All three men on board were injured but survived, and they were rescued by the coast guard. Depressed by the news, Mrs. Skaer and the pilot's father asked the coast guard to drag the sea bottom near Palos Verdes Peninsula. Reports of aircraft wreckage in the kelp beds off of the peninsula on August 5 were checked out and dismissed.

Mrs. Dorothy Skaer, in desperation, consulted a spiritual medium, who claimed that her husband would be found in the hills east of Los Angeles. Volunteer hikers and equestrians scoured the San Jose, La Puente and Chino Hills without result. Just when the public memory was beginning to wane regarding this case, an aircraft tire was found floating some 280 miles off San Diego. The recovered tire did not match the type used on the Northrop 3A. In mid-January 1936, a body was found floating off Santa Monica with trousers still on it and with a distinctive belt buckle. Families and friends thought that the mystery had been solved, but the body turned out to be that of man whose car had plunged over a 150-foot cliff into the ocean near Point Mugu on January 5, 1936. In June 1936, Mrs. Dorothy Skaer decided to remarry and continue with her life.

What happened to the Northrop 3A and its pilot, First Lieutenant Arthur H. Skaer Jr., may never be known unless the remains of his aircraft are found by chance off Palos Verdes Peninsula, Malibu or in deeper waters west of present-day LAX. There was much speculation at the time about the possible causes of the accident. Did the pilot initiate a spin from which he could not recover, or did he fly, as fishermen claimed, into the mists of aviation accident history?

During World War II, Douglas, Lockheed, North American, Northrop and Vultee were producing thousands of fighters, bombers, transports and trainers for the war effort. Delivering these aircraft to bases from which they were to be deployed created a logistics problem for which three basic modes were used. Partially assembled aircraft were shipped by rail across the country and by steam ships from the ports of Los Angeles and Long Beach. The most efficient way to deploy factory-fresh warplanes was to fly them to the operational air bases where they were most needed. To accomplish this method of delivery, the Army Air Transport Command established a spinoff, the Ferry Command, whose members would fly directly from the factory to operational squadrons within the continental United States or to ports of embarkation, where the aircraft would be shipped overseas for use in combat theaters across the globe.

The Ferry Command pilots had to be able to fly a variety of aircraft types, some of which required specialized training, such as multi-engine or high-performance fighters. The regulations of the command were straightforward: no night flying, no deliveries in bad weather (IFR) and deliveries were only to be made under (VFR) visual flight rules. There was only one pressing problem in 1942–43, and that was the lack of pilots available to accomplish the ferrying mission. One way to ease the pressure on the army air force was to find qualified pilots where the military had not considered before: using qualified female pilots.

Thanks to the efforts of Jacqueline Cochrane and Nancy Harkness Love, the Women Airforce Service Pilots (WASP) organization was established by the order of air force commanding general Henry "Hap" Arnold on August 5, 1943. Almost 25,000 women applied to join the WASP program. Only 1,830 were accepted, and of those, 1,074 became WASPs.

Some of the women who were accepted into the WASP program already had a pilot's license, and this was an obvious plus. Most of those who entered the program were in their twenties, but a few of the WASPs were older, and one these, in her early thirties, was Gertrude V. Tompkins. A New Jersey native, Ms. Tompkins grew up in a well-to-do family. She had two sisters, attended college and had a boyfriend who joined the Royal Air Force prior to the U.S. entry into World War II. Sadly, he was killed in action, and his loss may have motivated Gertrude to learn to fly and, later, apply her skills to aid in the war effort. Her sister, Elizabeth Tompkins-Whittall, said that Gertrude had a speech impediment, a stutter, but once she learned to fly, the stutter disappeared.

Gertrude was assigned to WASP training class 43-7 (July 1943) and graduated with flying colors. Upon joining the Ferry Command, she asked to fly fighter aircraft and, as a result, attended "fighter school," where she qualified on the North American Aviation P-51 Mustang, the hottest pursuit aircraft in the army air force inventory. Her friends and fellow WASPs called her "Tommy." She exuded confidence and spoke often of her duty to do all that she could to sustain the war effort. Gertrude "Tommy" Tompkins also became Mrs. Tompkins-Silver in 1944, when she secretly married New York businessman and U.S. Army Master Sergeant Henry Silver. WASP pilots were forbidden to marry while in service, but several did, keeping their nuptials a closely guarded secret.

On October 26, 1944, fifty pilots from the Sixth Ferrying Group arrived at the North American Aviation factory at Mines Field (LAX) to fly factory-fresh P-51D-25 (Block 25 with bubble canopy). Forty P-51Ds were to fly to Coolidge Field, and two

WASP Gertrude V. Tompkins-Silver disappeared on October 26, 1944, after taking off from Mines Field on a cross-country ferrying mission. *Courtesy the Whittall-Scherfee family.*

were to be sent to Kingman Field in Arizona. Nine other P-51Ds were to be flown to Palm Springs, California. Departures from Mines Field began at 3:00 p.m. for those aircraft en route to Arizona, and the Palm Springs–bound P-51Ds began departing at 3:30 p.m. However, there was a problem reported in the final flight of three Mustangs. P-51D-25 44-15669, assigned to WASP Gertrude V. Tompkins, was experiencing a canopy locking problem. The problem was reported fixed by 3:50 p.m., and the final flight of three took off from runway 25 Left at about 4:00 p.m. The first two P-51s were seen shortly after departure as they headed east over Imperial Highway flying on Green Airway 5 direct to Palm Springs Army Airfield in Riverside County. The last P-51D to depart Mines Field was flown by Tompkins, and her aircraft was not noticed on the eastbound leg of the flight.

The weather at the time of departure was one to three miles visibility in haze, with a fog bank along the coastline. When eight of the nine P-51s arrived at Palm Springs, the pilots assumed that Tompkins was still having canopy problems and that she had returned to Mines Field. No phone call was made to confirm this, and through a series of errors, Gertrude Tompkins was not posted missing until October 30, 1944. A search effort was launched the next day and continued for two weeks, with the primary focus being on the Banning Pass between San Bernardino and Palm Springs. Several vessels were used to search the choppy waters of Santa Monica Bay, but no trace of the shiny, polished aluminum fighter plane could be found. Next of kin were notified, though news media gave scant attention to the disappearance. A notice to airmen was posted to be on the lookout for the missing P-51, but there was a war going on, and the Tompkins case was quickly forgotten, except by those who loved and missed her.

WASP pilots were not in the military, although they wore uniforms and practiced military-style discipline and protocols. WASPs were not issued dog tags, did not have insurance and earned low wages, and if illness or death occurred, there was no coverage for medical attention or burial. If a WASP family did not have the funds, sister WASPs would chip in to cover the costs. Gertrude "Tommy" Tompkins-Silver was one of thirty-eight WASPs to lose their lives in service to our nation, but she is also the only WASP missing and unaccounted for.

Duncan Miller, an army Ferry Command pilot and friend of Gertrude's, was heartbroken to learn of her loss, as he freely admitted years later in an interview that he had a crush on her. He was especially shocked to learn that she was married. Her husband, Henry Silver, was truly devastated at the loss of the beloved wife and fly girl whom he adored. According to members of his family, Mr. Silver died a few years after Gertrude's death of sorrow and loneliness.

What exactly happened to Gertrude Tompkins-Silver may never be known, but it has been speculated that her canopy-locking device was an issue and that she may have become momentarily distracted during takeoff, allowing the Mustang to climb at too steep an angle, causing it to stall. Without enough altitude, Gertrude would not have been able to recover before crashing into the Pacific Ocean west of Dockweiler County Beach. There is some evidence supporting this scenario, and it comes from a then twelve-year-old boy, Frank Jacobs, who was fishing from the Manhattan Beach Pier. From his spot on the pier, Frank heard an engine seem to sputter, looked up and saw a P-51 Mustang descending in the haze. Frank still remembers how he called attention to the crash by notifying a man at the bait kiosk. The response of old man was, "Shut up, kid, and go home. They probably already know about it at the field."

When Frank went home and told his father about what happened, his dad waited to see what might appear in the local newspaper. When nothing appeared in the following days, Frank's credibility was smashed. The Jacobs family moved shortly thereafter, and the incident was forgotten, until an article appeared in a local newspaper that jogged Frank's memory. He then contacted the author, who at the time was the coordinator for the search for Ms. Tompkin's missing P-51D. The author interviewed Mr. Jacobs and later met him at the Manhattan Beach Pier, where he pointed out a possible point of impact for the P-51D on October 26, 1944. Mr. Jacobs, who earned a PhD at USC, is a highly respected aerospace engineer, now retired from Northrop Grumman Corporation.

The keen interest of Gertrude's grandniece, Laura Whittall-Scherfee, and her husband, Ken, helped to propel search efforts in Santa Monica Bay from 1997 to the present day. Ken and Laura became Gertrude's next-of-kin link and helped motivate volunteer search participants beginning in July–August 1999 and again in summer and fall of 2000 with the author, Jim Blunt and James Wadsley, who spearheaded the initial side-scan sonar searches west of Dockweiler County Beach. In 2001, a new search technology was added, using the sub-bottom profiler, produced by Imagenex and operated by a two-man team from Washington State. The September 11 tragedy stopped search efforts that had just started west of LAX, but they resumed the following year with no results. Coroner divers from San Bernardino County David Van Norman and John Croaker were also active in early operations.

Beginning in late summer 2003, Gary Fabian of UB88.org began to offer his expertise interpreting USGS multi-beam data and greatly expanded the theater of operations on SAMO Bay. A 2005 search produced two targets that seemed promising, but later examination revealed them to be wreckage of a small sailboat and powerboat that were located by hard-hat divers Eric Rosado and Karl Lutz, along with Tyler Fenton, the skipper of the dive vessel *Ranger*. Thanks to Frank Jacobs's eyewitness account, search efforts on Santa Monica Bay have been intensely focused in the area he thought the P-51D may have crashed, but the seabed in this search zone is covered in six to twelve feet of muck from the old Hyperion sewage treatment outfall short pipe (no longer used). Today, the plant, located in El Segundo, has pipes that deposit the treated sludge many miles off shore. Runoff from Ballona Creek near Marina Del Rey has further compounded the search problem by depositing sediments in the prime search area, which makes locating the remains of P-51D 44-15669 all but impossible without sub-bottom profiling or advanced magnetic anomaly detection (MAD) equipment.

HISTORIC AIRCRAFT WRECKS OF LOS ANGELES COUNTY

On Veterans Day 2008, a memorial gathering at the Proud Bird Restaurant near LAX hosted by U.S. Army Chaplin Captain Jeffery W. Clemens honored the memory of all thirty-eight WASP pilots who died while in service during World War II. Members of the Tompkins-Silver and Whittall-Scherfee families attended, both for the memorial and for the dedication of a bronze plaque honoring the service and loss of Gertrude Tompkins-Silver. The plaque is now on display at the Flight Path Museum at LAX. Among those present on November 11, 2008, were individuals willing to help fund the last large-scale search for P-51D 44-15669 on Santa Monica Bay to date. They included Gary Fabian, founder of UB88.org; Chris Killian, founder of the Missing Aircraft Search Team (MAST); and the author, founder of www.aircraftwrecks.com. These individuals and their respective teams agreed to cooperate and launch a five-day search effort beginning on October 2009. Gary Fabian had identified seventy-six targets in the Greater Santa Monica Bay area for the UB88.org and MAST teams to dive on, photo document and identify. Hopes were high that if Gertrude was not buried in the sediments and sludge of in-shore waters, her P-51D would be found. Knowing that aluminum is easily corroded in ocean salt water, the divers were hoping to find the 1,490-horsepower Packard-built Rolls Royce Merlin V-1650-7 engine, propeller blades, stainless steel parts, landing gear legs, six .50-inch machine guns, cockpit armor plate, armored windscreen or Plexiglas from the canopy. Pilot remains were not anticipated, as microorganisms consume both flesh and bone in the marine environment of Santa Monica Bay.

Volunteers came from across Los Angeles and Orange Counties and from across the country. The King Harbor Yacht Club opened its doors, and Bob Meistrall, the founder of Body Glove Wetsuits, donated his time and his seventy-two-foot vessel *The Disappearance* for daily use transporting divers and their gear to target locations from Redondo Beach to El Segundo. Ken and Laura Whittall-Scherfee were on board dive boats every day during the search effort, hoping that one of the teams would get lucky and find the elusive P-51D. Visibility in Santa Monica Bay varied greatly, from two to four feet up to ten to fifteen feet, depending on the dive location. Dive depths were as shallow as sixty-five feet and as deep as two hundred feet or more, requiring re-breathers, or scuba tanks with mixed gases. What divers found varied greatly: rock formations, a porcelain toilet, concrete blocks, boat anchors and other man-made debris dumped in the bay over the past hundred years. There were some aviation-related discoveries too: an aircraft drop tank in deep water and parts of a Cessna 210 that had ditched many years earlier from which all occupants escaped alive.

THE MISSING

As the 2009 search effort wound down, the sea state deteriorated, with onshore winds steadily increasing, making continued search operations both uncomfortable and dangerous. Intermittent searches are continuing on Santa Monica Bay, but at the time of this writing, there are no results to report concerning the Gertrude V. Tompkins-Silver case.

Since the 2009 search, Elizabeth Whittall, Gertrude's last surviving sister, passed away at age 101, but the Whittall-Scherfee family is still hopeful that remnants of Gertrude Tompkins-Silver's P-51D will eventually be found and that the final resting place of the only missing WASP will be known. Laura Whittall-Scherfee, the grandniece of Gertrude Tompkins-Silver, traveled to Washington to receive the Congressional Gold Medal in March 2010. The ceremony honoring all WASPs also included the reading of the names of the thirty-eight WASPs who had lost their lives in service to our nation, and a "missing man" flyover of the U.S. Air Force Memorial moved everyone who witnessed it.

Another disappearance occurred on April 21, 1945, when North American Aviation AT-6C 42-32900 departed Kingman Army Air Field at 9:25 a.m. en route to Mines Field (LAX) via Palmdale, California, with a crew of two on board. The flight was made in instrument conditions because of bad weather, with ceilings reported at two hundred feet AGL. When the T-6C failed to arrive at Mines Field, a search was initiated. After two weeks of searching with no results, it was speculated that the T-6C may have overflown Mines Field in the fog and possibly run out of fuel over the Pacific Ocean. The mystery of 42-32900 and the fate of its crew—Captain Fred A. Pugh, pilot, and First Lieutenant Thomas F. Turner, passenger—has yet to be solved.

While some searches can extend for weeks, months, years and beyond, others are resolved quickly. This is especially true when the pilot files a flight plan. Ronald C. Hall was working in Taft, California, as a petroleum engineer trainee when he disappeared on November 21, 1952, while flying home to stay with his parents in Montebello. His flight plan aided searchers because he described his route over the Tejon Pass, following Highway 99 (I-5) and expecting to land at El Monte Airport in Los Angeles County within an hour and forty-five minutes of his departure. The weather along the flight route included stratus clouds in and around the Los Angeles Basin. When he failed to arrive as scheduled, Mr. Hall was posted missing and a search was initiated. The Civil Air Patrol and the Los Angeles County Sheriff's Department Aero Squadron began search flights for the missing Luscombe 8A Silvaire, N1912K. The Silvaire was an all-aluminum, high-wing two-

The tail of Luscombe 8A N1912K protrudes from the chaparral east of Mount Harvard in the Angeles National Forest. *Courtesy Sewell F. Griggers.*

seat light aircraft, powered by a sixty-five-horsepower Continental A65 four-cylinder engine. With a cruising speed of 104 miles per hour, the Silvaire was considered to be a stable and easy-to-fly light aircraft, a hallmark of the post–World War II boom in private flying.

The morning of November 25, 1952, was clear with good visibility, and just before 10:00 a.m., a sheriff's department aircraft spotted the wreckage of the missing Luscombe 8A in the upper reaches of Big Santa Anita Canyon. The crash site was north of the town of Sierra Madre and east of Mount Harvard. When the sheriff's search and rescue team arrived with U.S. Forest Service rangers, they found Mr. Hall deceased in the crumpled cockpit of his aircraft. Weather, it was later determined, was a factor in the accident.

Another Luscombe 8A N1542K went missing on June 8, 1953, during a flight from Apple Valley Airport in San Bernardino County to Compton Airport in Los Angeles County with one man on board. The search for this errant aircraft lasted several weeks without result. At this time, there were more than a half dozen aircraft listed as missing in the state of California. During a search for another missing light aircraft on March 26, 1954, the wreckage of N1542K was found in Bailey Canyon, near the West Fork of Little Santa Anita Canyon, just a few miles from the crash site of Luscombe

8A N1912K. Both Luscombe accidents shared one thing in common: weather was a factor. That they were both Luscombe 8As and crashed in the same general area is purely coincidental.

Military cross-country training flights are an essential part of maintaining aircrew readiness and effectiveness. These flights are made day or night, in good weather and in bad. They are often referred to as proficiency flights, and they are required by all military service branches.

First Lieutenant Richard M. Theiler and First Lieutenant Paul D. Smith were both good friends, and they were members of the air force reserve assigned to the Air Defense Command (ADC) Seventeenth Tow Target Squadron at Yuma County Airport, Arizona.

On October 14, 1955, they were tasked to fly a navigational proficiency mission that included at least two hours of night flying for each pilot. They departed Yuma at 4:00 p.m. and flew nonstop to the air force base at LAX, arriving at 5:05 p.m. Their instructions required that they have dinner, go to bed early and depart LAX by 2:00 a.m. in order to accomplish the night portion of their mission.

The young lieutenants were flying an air force Lockheed T-33A trainer, commonly called the T-Bird. It was the standard advanced jet trainer for both the air force and the navy. More than 6,500 were produced between 1947 and 1957, and a few are still in foreign military use today. The T-33A carried a crew of two in a tandem arrangement and was powered by the 4,600-pound-thrust Allison J33-A-23 jet engine. The wing span is thirty-eight feet, ten and a half inches, and length is thirty-seven feet, nine inches, with a gross weight of 11,965 pounds. On the wing tips of the T-33A were two large aerodynamic fuel tanks, each one containing 165 gallons of JP-4. The escape system relied on early cannon shell charged ejection seats.

The handling characteristics of the T-Bird were, as its nickname implied, like a jet sports car capable of speeds up to 543 miles per hour.

At 2:15 a.m. on October 15, T-33A, USAF serial number 51-9227, departed LAX on an instrument (IFR) flight plan back to Yuma, Arizona. The weather conditions included light winds and stratus, with cloud tops to 3,500 feet. LAX control requested that the crew report at two thousand feet AGL. No transmission was heard from 51-9227, and when it failed to arrive at Yuma County Airport, it was reported missing, at about 4:45 a.m. At 8:30 a.m., a coast guard cutter reported finding an oil slick fifteen miles west of LAX. Analysis later showed that it contained traces of jet fuel. Also participating in the search was air force first lieutenant Thomas Theiler, brother of one of the missing pilots.

Lockheed T-33A in air force markings similar to 51-9227 that disappeared en route from LAX to Yuma, Arizona, on October 15, 1955, with a crew of two on board. *Photo courtesy American Aviation Historical Society.*

On October 19, a lifeguard assigned to Dockweiler County Beach reported finding a landing gear strut with a tire attached. It was later confirmed to have come from a T-33A and that it had been in the water for only a few days. No further wreckage was found, and the search was suspended on October 20, 1955. The missing T-33A was soon forgotten about, except by the Theiler and Smith families, who were left to wonder what caused the T-33A to crash and where the wreck had come to rest on the bottom of the bay.

In 1955, LACSD captain Sewell Griggers added the T-33A to the Z list of missing aircraft thought to be within Los Angeles County. When the author visited Mr. Griggers in his Compton home in 1968 to interview him about aircraft crash sites he had visited during his long career with the sheriff's department, he provided a copy of the Z list that would, years later, be key to an important discovery beneath the waters of Santa Monica Bay.

Another Lockheed T-33A would find its way onto the Z List on February 28, 1959, when an air force flight with a crew of two went missing on a flight from Randolph AFB in Texas en route to March AFB in Riverside County. The pilot was Major Thomas W. Greenwood, and his back seat passenger was Colonel Harry G. Moseley, who had made a speech at the Randolph School of Aviation Medicine and was returning to March AFB following a fuel stop at El Paso AFB in Texas. Major Greenwood made five position reports during the last leg of the flight, with the final contacts being made from twenty-nine thousand feet over the Riverside Low Frequency range at 8:34 p.m. What happened in the next twenty-two minutes tragically led to the loss of T-33A 56-3683 at 8:56 p.m., when it disappeared from the RAPCON radar at March AFB. It was later determined that the RAPCON controller was communicating with 56-3683 while looking at another aircraft on his radar screen. Unfortunately, this kind of error would be repeated many times in the years to come, resulting in the needless loss of many lives.

At sunrise on March 1, 1959, an air and ground search was initiated. However, the rescue effort was canceled after fourteen days of intensive searching with no results. It was surmised that the T-33A had struck a mountain when the RAPCON controller directed Major Greenwood to execute a right turn at 8,000 feet. Heavy snow blanketed all of the high peaks in Southern California until the spring melting began. No new aircraft wreckage was reported until June 25, 1959, when a private pilot reported scattered shines on the west flank of 10,064-foot Mount San Antonio (Old Baldy). Captain Sewell Griggers of the Los Angeles County Sheriff's Department flew a department Bell 47 helicopter to investigate the reported shines and discovered scattered wreckage of the missing USAF T-33A T-Bird.

The T-33A had struck the mountain five hundred feet higher than expected, indicating that Major Greenwood saw the snow-covered ridge in the last seconds and pulled up, but not in time. The T-Bird did not burn, and although it was broken up, it was not smashed. One of the first air force rescue personnel to reach the crash site was Master Sergeant Robert Koch. He was flown to a saddle between West and East Mount San Antonio by helicopter and from there began the arduous hike down to the T-33A wreckage. Master Sergeant Koch was assigned to assist the Los Angeles County Coroner in removing the remains of Major Thomas W. Greenwood Jr. and Colonel Harry G. Moseley. Once that grim task was accomplished, the scattered wreckage had to be examined, photographed and marked with yellow Xs. The bright yellow paint was applied to parts of the T-33A and to large rock formations nearby so that passing airmen would not report the wreckage as that of an unknown or missing aircraft. The entire tail section and empennage was intact, but there was no way to safely recover it. In 1959, no helicopter was available that could hover at more than eight thousand feet and safely lift a tail assembly off the mountain. With recovery not an option, three air force men pushed the tail over a precipice into the steep canyon below, where it can still be seen today.

HISTORIC AIRCRAFT WRECKS OF LOS ANGELES COUNTY

Starboard wing with air force markings from Lockheed T-33A 56-3683, posted missing on February 28, 1959, and not located until June 25, 1959. *Photo by Pat J. Macha.*

Knowing the exact location of T-33A 56-3683 became the goal of Project Remembrance Team members Chris LeFave and Ryan Gilmore. In October 2010, Chris flew a recon mission with Ryan as an observer. Helped by the complete absence of snow on Mount San Antonio, they were able to spot the scattered wreckage of the T-Bird, albeit on a forbidding piece of real estate. Nonetheless, Chris LeFave, accompanied by the author's son, Pat J. Macha, was able to reach the crash site during a grueling fourteen-hour trek in late June 2011. What Pat and Chris found as they photo documented the T-33A included the disarmed ejection seats, sections of wing emblazoned with "USAF" and a section of fuselage with the serial number 56-3683, confirming that they were at the February 10, 1959 crash site. Before heading back up the mountain, Chris and Pat took some time to remember both air force officers who had died in this accident, as well as the next of kin they had left behind.

Another Z list aircraft was a Beechcraft Bonanza N7206B that disappeared on May 15, 1960, en route from Las Vegas, Nevada, to Van Nuys Airport in the San Fernando Valley with four persons on board. The Bonanza was painted white with red trim, which was considered a high-visibility paint scheme. The weather at the time was good over the deserts, but the usual May/June gloom, with stratus clouds up to nine thousand feet, was hanging about the Greater Los Angeles Basin and covering even the higher reaches of the San Gabriel Mountains.

N7206B departed Las Vegas at 11:00 a.m., with Mr. Ralph Quartaroli at the controls. Also on board were Mr. and Mrs. Ross Perrino and Mrs. Jayne Bridger Liberace, divorced from noted violinist George Liberace. The Bonanza cruised at about 170 miles per hour and was expected to arrive at Van Nuys at about 2:00 p.m. Once N7206B was posted missing, the Civil Air Patrol launched an intensive search operation lasting several weeks and limited search flights continuing on weekends for more than a month after that. Relatives of Mrs. Perrino continued the search at their own expense both in the air and on the ground. A reward of $6,000 was offered, and the Los Angeles County Sheriff's Department Aero Squadron received $1,000 to defray the costs for additional search flights.

With the passage of time, the mystery deepened. Days became weeks and then months, and still no trace of the Beechcraft had been found in the usual approaches to the Los Angeles Basin. The Cajon Pass was the route described in Mr. Quartaroli's flight plan, but the Soledad Pass and the Newhall Passes were checked as well. All high mountain peaks and ridges were searched multiple times, and the areas that were cloud enshrouded on May 15 were scoured, too, when the weather improved a few days later.

Finally, the discovery of N7206B came when least expected. Two U.S. Forest Service rangers and a Pasadena-area attorney were hiking down from the old Red Box Forest Service Station toward Valley Forge Campground when one of the rangers noticed something through the dense undergrowth just off the north side of the trail. Closer examination revealed the unburned remains of the missing Beechcraft Bonanza. It was November 28, 1960, and the next day, the remains of the victims were recovered and carried out on stretchers by members of a local search and rescue team. All the grieving families of the missing were finally rendered a measure of peace and closure.

How did the Bonanza get into the near bottom of a deep canyon behind Mount Wilson? Had the pilot crossed most of the ridges of the San Gabriel Mountains in the clouds and started his descent into the Los Angeles Basin just minutes too soon? Had he come via the Cajon Pass as planned, flying west under the dense cloud cover, only to fly up the west fork of the San Gabriel River? The Beechcraft had not collided with a mountain, but it had hit tall trees, shearing off one wing before crashing into the undergrowth three miles below the Red Box Station. The wristwatches on two of the victims stopped at 1:36 p.m. exactly, indicating that all on board had died instantly. Still, questions remained regarding $38,000 in luxury jewelry not recovered from the crash site. In early December 1960, the jewelry issue was still not resolved. Rangers suggested that packrats may have absconded with the jewels and other items that were still being sought, but two men's wallets and some jewelry had been recovered by November 30. Members of the rescue team marked the Bonanza's fuselage, tail and wings with orange *X*s. Within two years, most of the wreckage had been removed, reducing N7206B to a micro site made invisible today by the dense growth of chaparral.

April is said to be the cruelest month, but in Los Angeles County, the month of May accounts for more fatal aircraft accidents. No storms, no gale-force winds—just stratus clouds from the cool Pacific Ocean driven inland by a westerly flow of air. The stratus may hang along the coast or stretch inland almost one hundred miles, flooding the valleys and canyons with fog between 1,500 feet to an average of 2,500 feet and often higher. Flying in these relatively benign conditions is not usually a problem for IFR pilots, but for those airmen not instrument rated, scud running is their only choice. Some VFR pilots have been successful scud runners throughout their flying careers. Skill and luck may have seen them through, but not always, even for those who had a special way or trick to beat the weather.

On May 5, 1978, a Piper PA-18 with only the pilot on board was flying from Mesa, Arizona, to Cable, his home airport, located in San Bernardino County in the city of Upland. The weather along his flight route was fine except when he tried to enter the Greater Los Angeles Basin and the adjoining valleys of the Inland Empire, which were covered by stratus clouds up to 3,500 feet MSL. The pilot had told friends that he had a special way of getting into Cable Airport while flying in marginal VFR conditions. When he failed to arrive home, he was posted missing, and an extensive aerial search was initiated, especially focused on his flight route, which should have followed Interstate 10 through the Banning Pass and on to Cable Airport. The San Gabriel and San Bernardino Mountains in San Bernardino and Los Angeles Counties were scoured as well, especially on the south-facing slopes. After several weeks, the search efforts were scaled back for the missing Piper Super Cub, a high-wing, fabric-covered, two-seat tail dragger. The Super Cub was itself a good search airplane. Popular with hunters and fishermen, it had also served with army and air force as a trainer and observation aircraft. Rugged and dependable, the Super Cub could take off and land in a very limited area, and it can be fitted with floats in areas where lakes and rivers are the norm.

Several of the missing pilot's friends continued the search in their spare time without result until April 15, 1979, when his best friend got lucky flying over an area he had examined many times before, but this time the light was just right. The crash site was located on the west slope of 3,422-foot Potato

Mountain just west of the Mount Baldy Road. There is a road to the top of the mountain that is well used by hikers and mountain bikers, who enjoy the fine views from its summit. How could a white airplane with red trim remain invisible for eleven months? In June 2010, thanks to Ryan Gilmore, the author hiked with George Petterson and Bruce Guberman to the crash site at 3,380 feet MSL. The Super Cub's burned remains were hidden from view underneath the chaparral where the plane came to rest. The post-impact fire destroyed the fabric and the emergency locator transmitter but did not burn off the concealing undergrowth! The many visitors to Potato Mountain were within a few hundred feet of a missing aircraft, with the remains of the pilot still on board, and did not know it. The missing pilot's friends had continued to search the area near the mouth of San Antonio Canyon for a reason, as it was sometimes used by their friend as his back door to reach Cable Airport in marginal weather conditions. The efforts of a few good friends also brought closure to this missing pilot's parents.

In May 2009, Gary Fabian began using the latest USGS multi-beam survey data for Santa Monica Bay to identify anomalies that might be aircraft wreckage. After hundreds of hours of study and interpretation, Gary mapped seventy-six targets, one of which appeared in the area identified by Frank Jacobs as being considered for the October 26, 1944 Tompkins-Silver P-51D loss. On the morning of May 20, 2009, the UB88.org dive team—consisting of Captain Ray Arntz, skipper of the *Sundiver II*; Captain Kyaa Day Heller; Kendall Raine; and John Walker—proceeded from Marina Del Ray to the coordinates provided by Gary Fabian. The author, who had been apprised of this mission, waited patiently at home for some word. That afternoon, Gary Fabian called to say that the first diver to reach the target had returned to the surface with an electrifying one-word statement: "Airplane." Kyaa Day Heller had seen a concentrated debris field off Dockweiler County Beach and had taken photos of what she saw. Kendall Raine and John Walker also dove to the target, taking photos and mapping the crash site. Everyone was hopeful that the resting place of Gertrude Tompkins-Silver's P-51D Mustang fighter plane had been found at last.

Gary sent the crash site photos to the author, and in an instant, ecstasy turned to disbelief and then disappointment. Instead of the Packard Merlin V-1650-7 engine block associated with the P-51D, the author saw a turbine wheel and compressor tubes from a turbo-jet engine. The dive had been successful, as aircraft wreckage had been found, but what jet was this from? Back to the Z list of missing planes thought to be in SAMO Bay. The most likely candidate was the Lockheed T-33A, which had disappeared on the night of October 15, 1955. Positive proof would be needed before the authorities were to be notified, and that meant another dive in search of a small, preferably stainless steel part that would hopefully have the prefix number series for the T-33A aircraft. Those numbers were well known to the author, having visited a half dozen T-33 crash sites in the mountains and deserts of California. The T-33A prefix series included numbers 176, 177, 178 and so on.

The next dive was successful, with one particularly interesting part arriving on the deck of the *Sundiver II*. After a brief cleaning, the stainless steel piece revealed the numbers 178032L. The letter *L* was not for Lockheed but rather denoted the left side of the aircraft. Where was the part located on the T-33A, and what was its purpose? The Lockheed Aircraft Company maintenance manual had the answers the team needed. It was located on the left side of the T-33A nose, and it was a chute assembly channel for a .50-inch machine gun. The T-33A was designed to carry two nose-mounted .50-inch machines guns for weapons training, but they were rarely fitted. The gun mounting assemblies were in place, however, if needed.

How could we prove that this was the missing T-33A 51-9227? A search of military accident records found that no other air force Lockheed T-33A or navy TV-2/T-33B aircraft were known to have crashed in SAMO Bay. The wrecked turbo jet engine proved to be that of an Allison J-33-A-35. The document in the author's possession that would provide proof that a missing T-33A existed was the Los Angeles County Sheriff's Department's Z list—Z-307-975, provided to

First Lieutenant Richard M. Theiler, pilot of T-33A 51-9227. *Courtesy the Theiler and Morton families.*

the author by Captain Sewell Griggers in 1968. With all of the evidence compiled and ready, it was presented to the sheriff's department, where it was vetted, allowing the department to eventually notify the next of kin for First Lieutenant Richard M. Theiler and First Lieutenant Paul D. Smith. Since this was also a case involving missing military personnel, JPAC, the Joint POW and MIA Accounting Command, was also notified. It authorized a sheriff's department dive team to recover artifacts from the T-33A crash site to confirm the discovery made by the UB88.org team. Some of the parts recovered included a hydraulic accumulator and part of the J-33 engine.

First Lieutenant Paul D. Smith, copilot of T-33A 51-9227. *Courtesy the Smith family.*

Among the next of kin, there was a combination of joy and sorrow when the notifications arrived that the resting place of their loved ones had been found and confirmed. For some, the shock of the suffering and loss of October 16 were relived. The pain of the first weeks and months in October 1955–56 returned, and the sleepless nights were repeated again. But they soon abated, as it became a time to remember the fallen flyers and celebrate their lives. Since there had been no memorial service in 1955, some family members wanted a service to be held on the beach nearest the crash site. Theresa Theiler Morton, niece of the T-33A pilot Richard M. Theiler, spearheaded the planning and execution of a memorial service that was held at Dockweiler County Beach on March 5, 2010. The air force provided a color guard, complete with a twenty-one-gun salute and a flag ceremony. Volunteers provided their boats and yachts to carry next of kin to the waters above the T-33A crash site, where flower petals and tears mingled on the calm Pacific where two air force officers had lost their lives nearly fifty-five years earlier. Tom Theiler, whose brother, Richard, died in the T-33A crash, said, "To be here is to be near my beloved brother again, and that means so much to me now."

The UB88.org team and Project Remembrance Team helped to facilitate this day of reflection, prayer and camaraderie, along with dozens of volunteer helpers and facilitators. The Ken and Laura Whittall-Scherfee family saluted the discovery of the missing T-33A, saying, "Gertrude wasn't ready to be found yet, and we're very happy for the Theiler and Smith families. We hope that someday the wreck of Gertrude's P-51D will be found too."

Gary Fabian continues to study multi-beam data for suspicious anomalies that might warrant putting divers back into the waters of Santa Monica Bay. Mr. Fabian contacted the author in August 2014 to say that his data had led to the discovery of another aircraft in Santa Monica Bay off the coast of Malibu. The wreckage was confirmed to be that of a U.S. Navy Douglas F4D-1 Skyray jet fighter that crashed during a pre-delivery test flight on March 18, 1958. The accident occurred following an in-flight explosion at fifteen thousand feet 0.9 Mach. Douglas Aircraft Company test pilot Pete Colapietro was critically injured during the high-speed ejection. His parachute opened automatically, and his life was saved by a Douglas Aircraft Company float-equipped helicopter that landed on Santa Monica Bay carrying a rescue swimmer. At about the same time, a Santa Monica lifeguard boat arrived on the scene to take the injured test pilot to shore, where an ambulance was waiting. Mr. Colapietro's injuries caused his face to swell so much that his vision was limited to one eye. His arms were severely injured, with one being broken and the other mangled. He managed to pull the toggles that inflated his life vest, but he could not release the smoke canister or do anything else. Before being rescued, he was in the water for about forty-five minutes. Pete Colapietro spent ten weeks in the hospital before returning home for an extended recovery period.

When the F4D-1 hit the Pacific Ocean on March 18, 1958, its location was not known, but it is now. Positive identification of the Skyray was made by analyzing just one photo of the main landing gear leg and its oleo strut, which is unique to the F4D-1 Skyray. Sometimes the search for one missing aircraft leads to the discovery of another. Yet to be found are at least sixteen missing aircraft (eleven civilian and five military) believed to have crashed in the Santa Monica Bay. As searchers continue the hunt with the application of new technologies, the bay may yet relinquish its secrets.

GLOSSARY OF TERMS

AAB: Army Air Base
AAF: Army Air Field
AAHS: American Aviation Historical Society
ADC: Air Defense Command
AFB: Air Force Base
AGL: Above Ground Level
ANG: Air National Guard
ATC: Air Traffic Control
BLM: Bureau of Land Management
CAB: Civil Aeronautics Board
CAP: Civil Air Patrol
ELT: Emergency Locator Transmitter
FAA: Federal Aviation Administration
IFR: Instrument Flight Rules
ILS: Instrument Landing System
LACSD: Los Angeles County Sheriff's Department
MATS: Material Air Transport Command
MCAS: Marine Corps Air Station
MSL: Mean Sea Level
NAA: North American Aviation
NACA: National Advisory Committee for Aeronautics
NAS: Naval Air Station
NASA: National Aeronautics and Space Administration

GLOSSARY OF TERMS

NTSB: National Transportation Safety Board
RAPCON: Radar Approach Control
SAR: Search and Rescue
SBCSD: San Bernardino County Sheriff Department
TAC: Tactical Air Command
USAA: United States Army Aviation
USAAC: United States Army Corps
USAAF: United States Army Air Force
USAF: United States Air Force
USAFR: United States Air Force Reserve
USFS: United States Forest Service
USMC: United States Marine Corps
USMCR: United States Marine Corps Reserve
USN: United States Navy
USNR: United States Navy Reserve
VFR: Visual Flight Rules
VOR: Very High Frequency Omni-directional Range
WASP: Women Airforce Service Pilot

Abbreviated military aircraft designations: A (Attack), B (Bomber), C (Cargo), F (Fighter), G (Glider), H (Helicopter), J (Test), L (Liaison), O (Observation), P (Pursuit), Q (Drone), R (Reconnaissance), T (Trainer), X (Experimental), Y (Experimental)

BIBLIOGRAPHY

Books

Carl, Ann B. *A WASP Among Eagles: A Woman Military Test Pilot in World War II*. Washington, D.C.: Smithsonian Institution Press, 1999.

Ellis, Glenn Ellis. *Air Crash Investigation of General Aviation Aircraft*. Wyoming: Capstan Publications Inc., 1984.

Francillon, Rene J. *Lockheed Aircraft Since 1913*. London: Putnam & Company Ltd., 1982.

———. *McDonnell Douglas Aircraft Since 1920*. London: Putnam & Company Ltd., 1979.

Green, William, and Gerald Pollinger. *The Aircraft of the World*. London: Macdonald & Company Ltd., 1965.

Leadabrand, Russ. *A Guidebook to the San Gabriel Mountains of California*. Los Angeles, CA: Ward Ritchie Press, 1964.

Macha, Gary P. *Aircraft Wrecks in the Mountains and Deserts of California, 1908–1920*. Huntington Beach, CA: Archaeological Press, 1991.

———. *Aircraft Wrecks in the Mountains and Deserts of California, 1909–1996*. San Clemente, CA: INFO NET Publishing, 1997.

Macha, G.P., and Don Jordan. *Aircraft Wrecks in the Mountains and Deserts of California, 1909–2002*. Huntington Beach, CA: Archaeological Press, 1991.

Merlin, Peter W., and Tony Moore. *X-Plane Crashes*. North Branch, MN: Specialty Press, 2008.

BIBLIOGRAPHY

Miller, Jay. *The X-Planes: X-1 to X-45*. 3rd ed. Hinckley, UK: Midland Publishing, 2001.

Mireles, Anthony J. *Fatal Army Air Forces Aviation Accidents in the United States, 1941–1945*. Vol. 1, *Introduction: January 1941–June 1943*. Jefferson, NC: McFarland & Company, 2006.

———. *Fatal Army Air Forces Aviation Accidents in the United States, 1941–1945*. Vol. 3, *August 1944–December 1945, Appendices, Indexes*. Jefferson, NC: McFarland & Company, 2006.

———. *Fatal Army Air Forces Aviation Accidents in the United States, 1941–1945*. Vol. 2, *July 1943–July 1944*. Jefferson, NC: McFarland & Company, 2006.

Robinson, John W. *Trails of the Angeles: 100 Hikes in the San Gabriels*. Berkeley, CA, 1984.

Swanborough, Gordon, and Peter M. Bowers. *United States Military Aircraft Since 1909*. Great Britain: Putnam Aeronautical Books, 1989. Originally published Washington, D.C.: Smithsonian Institution Press, 1989.

———. *United States Navy Aircraft Since 1911*. Great Britain: Putnam Aeronautical Books, Conway Maritime Press Ltd., 1990. Originally published Washington, D.C.: Smithsonian Institution Press, 1989.

Taylor, John W.R., and Gordon Swanborough. *Civil Aircraft of the World*. New York: Charles Scribner's Sons, Jan Allen Ltd., 1974.

Veronico, Nicholas A., Ed Davies, Donald B. McComb Jr. and Michael B. McComb. *Wreckchasing 2: Commercial Aircraft*. Castro Valley, CA: Pacific Aero Press, 1996.

Veronico, Nicholas, Ed Davies, A. Kevin Grantham, Robert A. Kropp, Enrico Massagili, Donald B. McComb, Michael B. McComb, Thomas William McGarry and Walt Wentz. *Wreckchasing 101: A Guide to Finding Crash Sites*. Charleston, SC: Stance & Speed, 2011.

White, William Sanford. *Santa Catalina Island Goes to War: World War II, 1941–1945*. City of Industry, CA: White Limited Editions, 2002.

Williams, Nick, and Steve Ginter. *Naval Fighters Number Thirteen: Douglas F4D Skyray*. Simi Valley, CA: Steve Ginter, 1986.

Young, Donald J. *Wartime Palos Verdes*. Palos Verdes, CA: self-published, 1984.

INTERVIEWS

Beam, Fred. Interviews by the author, 1968–69.

Butters, Marylynn Winkler. Interview by author, 2012.

Gates, Elgin F. Interviews by author, 1995–2009.

BIBLIOGRAPHY

Griggers, Sewell F. Interviews by author, 1968–70.
Jacobs, Frank. Interview by author, 2006.
Kofahl, James. Interview by author, 1984.
Matich, Stephen. Interview by author, 2014.
McGregor, Scotty. Interview by author, 1968–69.
Peltzer, Milo. Interviews by author, 2013–14.
Petterson, George. Interviews by author, 1999–2014.
Wolford, Roy. Interview by author, 2002.

NEWSPAPERS

Herald Examiner.
Inglewood Daily News.
Long Beach Independent.
Los Angeles Times.
Pasadena Independent.
Redlands Daily Facts.
Riverside Press Enterprise.
San Bernardino Sun, High Desert.
San Bernardino Sun, Valley.
San Diego Evening Tribune.
South Bay Daily Breeze.

ARTICLE

Johnson, G., Lieutenant Colonel, USMC (Ret.). "To the Edge and Back." *Wings of Gold* (Spring 2000).

CIVILIAN ACCIDENT REPORT

Civil Aeronautics Board, National Transportation Safety Board, Northrop Aircraft, Inc. Accident report, October, 28, 1947.

BIBLIOGRAPHY

MILITARY ACCIDENTS REPORTS

Kirtland AFB, New Mexico HQAFSCJA.
Maxwell AFB, Alabama AFHRA/RSA.
Naval History and Heritage Command, Washington, D.C.
Naval Safety Center, Norfolk, Virginia.

WEBSITES

Freeman, Paul. Abandoned & Little-Known Airfields. http://www.airfields-freeman.com.

Fuller, Craig. Aviation Archaeological Investigation & Research (AAIR). http://www.aviationarchaeology.com.

Los Angeles County Sheriff's Department Aircraft Incident Reports, 1937–71.

Macha, G.P. Aircraft Wrecks in the Mountains and Deserts of the American West. www.aircraftwrecks.com.

National WASP World War II Museum, Avenger Field, Sweetwater, Texas. http://waspmuseum.org.

Western Museum of Flight, Zamperini Field, Torrance, California. http://www.wmof.com.

Westin, Larry. "United Airliner Forced Down." SCV History, May 29, 2012. http://www.scvhistory.com/scvhistory/westin_n73102.htm.

VIDEO

Braverman Productions. *Broken Wings*. VHS /DVD, 2001.
Macha, G. Pat. *Wreck Finding: Lost but Not Forgotten*. VHS/DVD, 1995.

INDEX

INDEX

INDEX

INDEX

INDEX

INDEX

Wilson, Howard L., Second Lieutenant 58

Winkler-Butters, Marylynn 44

Winkler, Norman C. 41

Wolford, Roy L. 69

World War I 18

World War II 23, 30, 32, 33, 37, 45, 48, 51, 55, 58, 59, 61, 65, 66, 67, 69, 71, 73, 82, 113, 114, 118, 120

Wrightwood 48, 107

Y

Yoakley, Bill 88

Z

Zimmerman, John O., Pharmacist Mate First Class 66

Z list 128

Zwick, Charles C., Second Lieutenant 39

ABOUT THE AUTHOR

G. Pat Macha was born in Santa Monica, California. He is a graduate of Long Beach State College, with a BA in history and a minor in geography, as well as an MA from Azusa Pacific University. He taught at Hawthorne High School for thirty-five years, is married and is a father of two, with five grandchildren. He has authored five books on aircraft accidents in California and is a well-received speaker on aviation safety and accident histories. Pat has been documenting crash sites throughout California in remote locations for fifty-one years, and he has hiked to or flown over more than 150 crash sites in Los Angeles County. Since 1996, along with the Project Remembrance Team, he has assisted next of kin in visiting crash sites. To learn more about his work, visit www.aircraftwrecks.com.

Visit us at
www.historypress.net
....
This title is also available as an e-book

www.ingramcontent.com/pod-product-compliance
Lightning Source LLC
Chambersburg PA
CBHW060654150426
42813CB00053B/971